# Learning Magento Theme Development

Create visually stunning and responsive themes to customize the appearance of your Magento store

**Richard Carter**

**PACKT PUBLISHING**

open source*
community experience distilled

BIRMINGHAM - MUMBAI

# Learning Magento Theme Development

First published: August 2014

Production reference: 1130814

Published by Packt Publishing Ltd.
Livery Place
35 Livery Street
Birmingham B3 2PB, UK.

ISBN 978-1-78328-061-2

www.packtpub.com

Cover image by Benoit B (benoit.benedetti@gmail.com)

# Credits

**Author**
Richard Carter

**Reviewers**
Ray Bogman
Vali Lungu
Ankit Sharma
Mukund Thanki

**Acquisition Editor**
Sam Wood

**Content Development Editor**
Madhuja Chaudhari

**Technical Editors**
Kunal Anil Gaikwad
Ankita Thakur
Nachiket Vartak

**Copy Editors**
Roshni Banerjee
Adithi Shetty
Stuti Srivastava

**Project Coordinators**
Neha Bhatnagar
Akash Poojary

**Proofreaders**
Simran Bhogal
Ameesha Green

**Indexer**
Hemangini Bari

**Graphics**
Abhinash Sahu
Ronak Dhruv

**Production Coordinator**
Adonia Jones

**Cover Work**
Adonia Jones

# About the Author

**Richard Carter** is a web designer and frontend web developer based in Newcastle upon Tyne in the north east of England.

His experience includes many open source e-commerce and content management systems, including Magento, MediaWiki, WordPress, and Drupal. He has worked with clients such as the University of Edinburgh, University College Dublin, Directgov, NHS Choices, and BusinessLink.gov.uk.

He is the Creative Director at Peacock Carter Ltd (www.peacockcarter.co.uk), a web design and development agency based in the north east of England. He graduated from the University of Durham in Software Engineering, and currently lives in Newcastle upon Tyne. He blogs at http://www.earlgreyandbattenburg.co.uk and tweets as @RichardCarter and @PeacockCarter.

This is the author's seventh book. He has previously written *MediaWiki Skins Design*, *Magento 1.3 Theme Design*, *Magento 1.4 Theme Design*, *Joomla! 1.5 Templates Cookbook*, and *The Beginner's Guide to Drupal Commerce* by Packt Publishing. He was also a technical reviewer for *MediaWiki 1.1 Beginners Guide* and *Inkscape 0.48 Illustrator's Cookbook* by Packt Publishing and *The Definitive Guide To Drupal 7* by Apress.

In particular, my thanks are due to Matthew, who has kept Peacock Carter on track while I was focusing on this book! Also, thanks to my family and friends, and Anna, whose constant support is much appreciated.

# About the Reviewers

**Ray Bogman** is an IT professional and Magento evangelist from the Netherlands. He started working with computers in 1983, as a hobby. In the past, he worked for KPN, a large Dutch Telecom company, as a senior security officer.

He was the CTO of Wild Hibiscus, Netherlands, until 2010. He is the founder of Yireo and was the business creator there until 2011. He is also the founder of Jira ICT and has been the CEO since 2005. He is also the CTO of SupportDesk B.V., which he co-founded in 2011.

At SupportDesk B.V., he is a Magento, Joomla!, OroCRM, Web/Server/Mobile performance specialist and security evangelist. His focus during the day is business development and training webmasters and consultants about the power of Magento, from the basics up to an advanced level. He has trained over 1000 Magento and over 750 Joomla experts worldwide since 2005. He has been a regular speaker at Magento events such as Magento Developers Paradise and Meet since 2009.

Besides work, his hobbies are snowboarding, running, going to the movies and music concerts, and loving his wife Mette and daughter Belize.

He was the reviewer of *Mastering Magento* in 2012 the e-book, *Mastering Magento* the video in 2013, *Mastering Magento Theme Design* in 2014, and *Magento Administration Guide* in 2014.

**Vali Lungu** is a frontend developer with more than 12 years of experience in the area of software development. He started as an agent in a cyber-crime fighting unit and went through most aspects of web development, which includes frontend and backend programming in anything from JavaScript to Python, and establishing and developing frontend software architectures for complex Magento projects.

Currently, he is leading the frontend development team in one of the top Magento companies in Germany. While working there, he got certified as a Magento Front end Developer and added e-commerce application development to his technical skills.

> I would like to thank my friend and colleague Vedran Subotić, one of the best Magento experts you can find, for his helping hand in the process of reviewing this book and for the way he's always ready to collaborate and put his awesome backend skills to work towards achieving awesome Magento projects and making the most of the framework.

**Ankit Sharma** loves to code. It's not only his profession, but one of his many diverse hobbies along with playing cricket, soccer, tennis (sometimes in real life), watching his favorite TV shows and movies, and of course participating in online blogs. Incidentally, he is also one of the friendliest and funniest people you will come across, and this makes him a joy to work with.

His skills and knowledge, combined with his personality, led him to conduct workshop seminars for his college peers to help them better understand the latest technologies. He also pioneered the online college course access at his college to make programming tools available to other students remotely.

While in college, he majored in Computer Engineering from Saurashtra University, India and pursued an MTech in Computer Engineering from Dharmsinh Desai University, India. He is the cofounder and VP of Engineering at CrowdClock now.

**Mukund Thanki** was born and raised at Porbandar. He lives in Vadodara, Gujarat, India now. He holds a Bachelor's degree in Electronics and Communications; however, by following his passion of programming, he dived into PHP and ultimately found himself at the shore of the most famous and robust platforms such as Magento and WordPress. He founded Pushkar Creations (`http://pushkarcreations.com/`), where he enjoys working on e-commerce and CMS websites and finding appropriate solutions for clients. He also loves to implement unique concepts on the Web. For example, he created an online pedigree system (`http://pedigreepickle.com/`), which is a social networking site for pet owners, run by his brother. While not playing with code, he enjoys nature at his farmhouse with his friends and brothers. He always makes time to watch great movies and he listens to music all the time. If you are dealing with Magento or WordPress and find yourself in the middle of the sea, you can be in touch by following him on twitter @mukkundthanki or like his page on Facebook `https://www.facebook.com/pushkarcreations/` or contact him directly at `mukkundthanki@gmail.com`.

# www.PacktPub.com

## Support files, eBooks, discount offers, and more

You might want to visit www.PacktPub.com for support files and downloads related to your book.

Did you know that Packt offers eBook versions of every book published, with PDF and ePub files available? You can upgrade to the eBook version at www.PacktPub.com and as a print book customer, you are entitled to a discount on the eBook copy. Get in touch with us at service@packtpub.com for more details.

At www.PacktPub.com, you can also read a collection of free technical articles, sign up for a range of free newsletters and receive exclusive discounts and offers on Packt books and eBooks.

http://PacktLib.PacktPub.com

Do you need instant solutions to your IT questions? PacktLib is Packt's online digital book library. Here, you can access, read and search across Packt's entire library of books.

## Why subscribe?

- Fully searchable across every book published by Packt
- Copy and paste, print and bookmark content
- On demand and accessible via web browser

## Free access for Packt account holders

If you have an account with Packt at www.PacktPub.com, you can use this to access PacktLib today and view nine entirely free books. Simply use your login credentials for immediate access.

# Table of Contents

# Preface

Magento is now the most popular e-commerce platform in the world, and distinguishing your store from others has become more important than ever.

This book introduces Magento theming to web designers and developers with a basic understanding of HTML and CSS upwards, who want to discover the secrets of theming Magento for both client projects and their own projects.

## What this book covers

*Chapter 1, Introduction to Magento and Magento Themes,* provides an introduction to the topic, including exploring what a Magento theme is, Magento theme terminology including Templates, Layouts, and Skins, and the Magento theme hierarchy.

*Chapter 2, Magento Theming Basics,* gets you started with your new Magento theme, from enabling a new theme in Magento to changing the logo, customizing the product watermark images, disabling Magento's caches, and using Magento's Template Path Hints tool, as well as creating a new Magento theme.

*Chapter 3, Magento Templates,* provides simple layout styling for your Magento theme, customizing your store's header and footer, and the search box, and covers how to add a static block to a template, as well as styling your checkout and cart page.

*Chapter 4, Magento Layout,* looks at adding a local.xml file to your theme, changing the default page template, adding a static block to a page using the Magento layout, changing the order of blocks in Magento's sidebar using layout, removing unnecessary blocks in Magento's sidebar, and adding a new products list to your store's home page.

*Chapter 5, Social Media and Magento*, covers integrating a Twitter feed with your Magento store, integrating a Facebook page with your Magento store, including social share buttons on your product pages to help increase your store's reach, and integrating product videos from YouTube with product listings.

*Chapter 6, Advanced Magento Theming*, explores adding a custom print style sheet for your Magento store, using locales to translate labels/phrases in your store, using @ font-face in Magento, styling Magento's layered navigation, creating a custom 404 "not found" error page, and using microformats for rich snippets to enhance search engine listings.

*Chapter 7, Magento Theming for Mobile and Tablet Devices*, walks the reader through how to use CSS media queries to create breakpoints for different device widths, making images responsive to your Magento theme, developing responsive navigation for your Magento theme, and adding mobile home page icons for Windows and Apple devices to your Magento theme.

*Chapter 8, Magento E-mail Templates*, covers hanging the default e-mail template logo to altering colors of the e-mail templates and altering variables in Magento e-mail templates, as well as adding static block content to your Magento e-mail templates.

# What you need for this book

You will need access to a working installation of Magento Community Edition 1.8 or newer, and your preferred code-editing software.

# Who this book is for

If you are a web designer or web developer who is familiar with XML, HTML, and CSS, who wants to learn the fundamental building blocks of creating a Magento theme, this book is for you. A basic understanding of PHP is helpful but not required.

# Conventions

In this book, you will find a number of styles of text that distinguish between different kinds of information. Here are some examples of these styles and an explanation of their meaning.

Code words in text, database table names, folder names, filenames, file extensions, pathnames, dummy URLs, user input, and Twitter handles are shown as follows: "In Magento, skin files are located in the `/skin/frontend/` directory."

A block of code is set as follows:

```
* {
margin:0;
padding:0;
}
img {
border:0;
vertical-align:top;
}
a {
color:#1e7ec8;
text-decoration:underline;
}
```

When we wish to draw your attention to a particular part of a code block, the relevant lines or items are set in bold:

```
* {
margin:0;
padding:0;
}
img {
border:0;
vertical-align:top;
}
a {
color:#1e7ec8;
text-decoration:underline;
}
```

**New terms** and **important words** are shown in bold. Words that you see on the screen, in menus or dialog boxes for example, appear in the text like this: "You might notice that there are many superfluous blocks in the sidebar, such as the **BACK TO SCHOOL** and **COMMUNITY POLL** blocks, which would not be required on a usual e-commerce website."

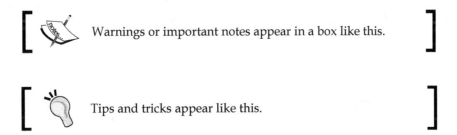

[ Warnings or important notes appear in a box like this. ]

[ Tips and tricks appear like this. ]

# Reader feedback

Feedback from our readers is always welcome. Let us know what you think about this book—what you liked or may have disliked. Reader feedback is important for us to develop titles that you really get the most out of.

To send us general feedback, simply send an e-mail to feedback@packtpub.com, and mention the book title via the subject of your message.

If there is a topic that you have expertise in and you are interested in either writing or contributing to a book, see our author guide on www.packtpub.com/authors.

# Customer support

Now that you are the proud owner of a Packt book, we have a number of things to help you to get the most from your purchase.

# Downloading the example code

You can download the example code files for all Packt books you have purchased from your account at http://www.packtpub.com. If you purchased this book elsewhere, you can visit http://www.packtpub.com/support and register to have the files e-mailed directly to you.

# Errata

Although we have taken every care to ensure the accuracy of our content, mistakes do happen. If you find a mistake in one of our books—maybe a mistake in the text or the code—we would be grateful if you would report this to us. By doing so, you can save other readers from frustration and help us improve subsequent versions of this book. If you find any errata, please report them by visiting http://www.packtpub.com/submit-errata, selecting your book, clicking on the **errata submission form** link, and entering the details of your errata. Once your errata are verified, your submission will be accepted and the errata will be uploaded on our website, or added to any list of existing errata, under the Errata section of that title. Any existing errata can be viewed by selecting your title from http://www.packtpub.com/support.

# Piracy

Piracy of copyright material on the Internet is an ongoing problem across all media. At Packt, we take the protection of our copyright and licenses very seriously. If you come across any illegal copies of our works, in any form, on the Internet, please provide us with the location address or website name immediately so that we can pursue a remedy.

Please contact us at copyright@packtpub.com with a link to the suspected pirated material.

We appreciate your help in protecting our authors, and our ability to bring you valuable content.

# Questions

You can contact us at questions@packtpub.com if you are having a problem with any aspect of the book, and we will do our best to address it.

# 1

# Introduction to Magento and Magento Themes

Magento is a popular, enterprise-level open source e-commerce platform used by hundreds of thousands of e-commerce businesses around the world. With ever increasing numbers of online stores competing for customers and income, it can pay off to invest in customizing your Magento store to set it apart from hundreds and thousands of other stores, and developing a custom Magento theme is the way to achieve this.

In this chapter, you will learn the following topics:

- What a Magento theme is and what Magento themes can do
- An overview of the default Magento themes in Magento
- An introduction to the Magento theme terminology
- How the Magento theme hierarchy works

## What is a Magento theme?

A Magento theme is simply a collection of files that tells Magento how to display your store to visitors. A Magento theme can consist of a collection of CSS, HTML, PHP, XML, and images, all of which contribute to the look and feel of your store.

Due to Magento's architecture and the design interface's hierarchy, Magento will fall back to base theme (discussed later in this chapter) that contain the files it requires if they are not present in the current theme. A Magento theme can consist of one or more of the previously mentioned files. It could be as simple as a logo file with the rest of your store's styling provided by a parent theme.

# Magento's default themes

In Magento Community Edition 1.8, Magento provides the following four themes:

- Default
- Blank
- iPhone
- Modern

# The default theme

Magento's default theme is perhaps, unsurprisingly, the theme that is enabled by default when you first install Magento, encompassing a clear header area with a search field and drop-down navigation for categories to be listed, a content area with sidebar(s), and a footer, as shown in the following screenshot:

The default theme's product page layout retains the header and footer styling of the home page layout, but the central content area is adapted to present the product information to customers, as shown in the following screenshot:

As you can see in the preceding screenshot, the product page provides a product image with the name, a brief description, and the price of the specific product towards the top of the page. Then, a more detailed description is provided in the next block.

 You might notice that there are many superfluous blocks in the sidebar, such as the **BACK TO SCHOOL** and **COMMUNITY POLL** blocks, which would not be required on a usual e-commerce website. These blocks help showcase how powerful Magento is to new developers and can be removed fairly easily.

# The category page layout

One of the next key views for your Magento store is the category page layout, which presents all the products grouped within a particular product category, as shown in the following screenshot:

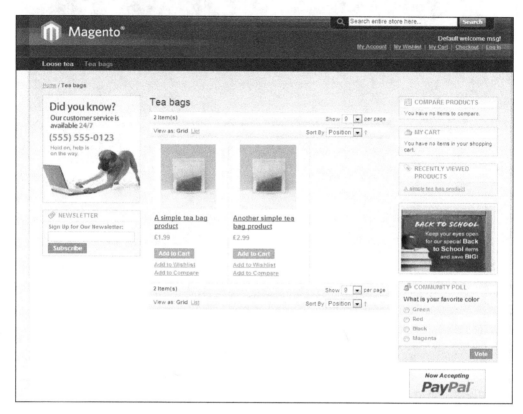

# The list mode layout

Magento presents products in two ways: in a grid (as shown in the preceding screenshot) and as a list, which you can select by clicking on the **List** option in the product grid, as shown in the following screenshot:

In the list mode, products within the selected category are displayed one above the other, as shown in the following screenshot:

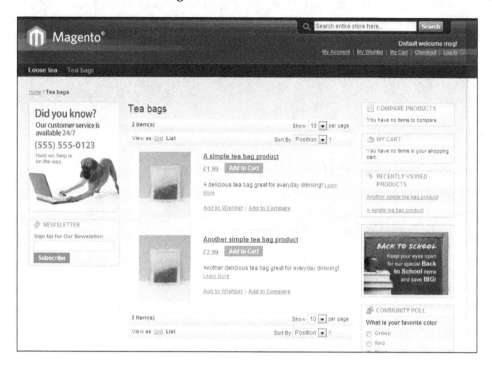

# Checkout

Finally, Magento's famous one-page checkout provides a well-structured checkout process for your customers, as shown in the following screenshot, maintaining the default theme's overall character:

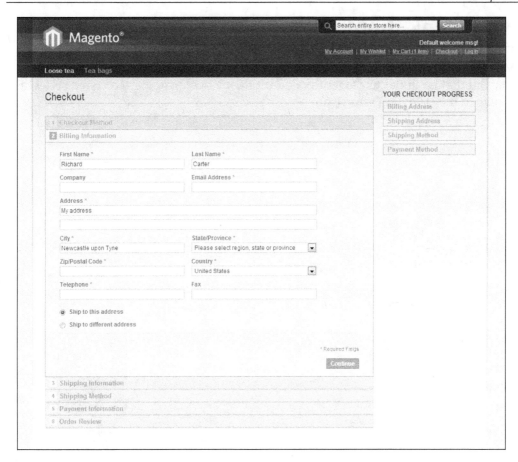

Next, you will see the additional Magento themes that come with Magento Community Edition 1.8 to cater to different needs for both customers and developers.

# The blank theme

The blank theme, as its name suggests, provides a very minimal approach to a Magento theme to allow a custom Magento theme to be built upon it, maintaining a layout that is similar to Magento's default theme but stripping the visual styles, as shown in the following screenshot:

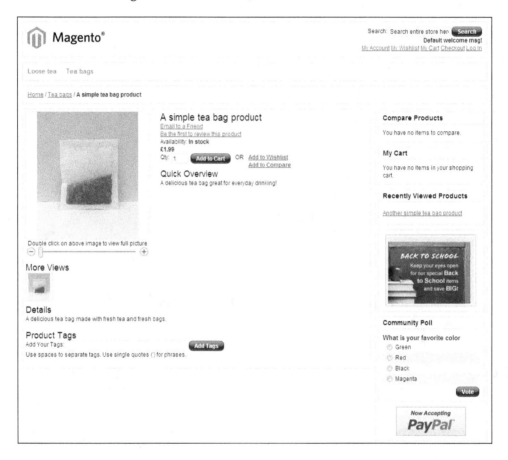

# The iPhone theme

The iPhone theme provides a more mobile-friendly theme for your Magento store, which can be switched on and off for specified devices. This view of the home page with the iPhone theme shows you how content is streamlined and slimmed down to help present the most relevant information to your customers on devices with limited screen space available, as shown in the following screenshot:

# The modern theme

Finally, the modern theme provides a full-fledged Magento theme that can be used as an alternative to the default theme, with a more contemporary look, as shown in the following screenshot:

These themes show you just the surface of the potential customizations you can make to your Magento store, and this book will guide you through some of the common changes made to Magento stores as well as some less common alterations you can make to improve your Magento theme.

# Magento terminology

As with many other open source technologies, Magento comes with its own terminology, which can be baffling to unfamiliar developers. This section identifies and defines some of the commonly used terms in the Magento theme development.

## Scope in Magento

Magento has the following four levels of scope that help define the level in your Magento store(s) at which settings are applied:

- **Global**: This refers to settings that affect the entire Magento installation.

- **Website**: This acts as the parent entity for one or more stores in the Magento terminology. Websites can be configured to share the customer data or not share any data at all.

- **Store (or store view group)**: These are the hierarchical children of Magento websites. Products and categories are managed at Magento's store level. A root category is configured for each Magento store, allowing multiple stores under the same website to have totally different catalog structures.

- **Store view**: A store needs one or more store views to appear in the frontend to customers so they are able to browse your store. The store view inherits the store's category and product information, and so the changes at the store view level are typically only cosmetic, changing the way the data is presented. The most common and likely implementation of multiple store views is to allow customers to navigate between two or more languages.

# Magento websites, stores, and store views

It is possible to run many different e-commerce stores from one Magento installation, and it's also possible to run separate stores on the same website (for example, a consumer store and a trade store that offers discounts to trade customers). The simplest of Magento websites, however, consists of a single website with a single store and single store view as follows:

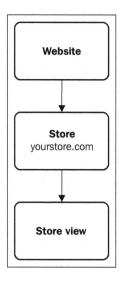

# Using multiple stores in Magento

The most common use of multiple stores in Magento is to build separate stores with their own inventories. For example, you could have one store, `veryverycoolt-shirts.com`, to sell t-shirts, and another, `veryverycoolcaps.com`, to sell baseball caps through the same installation of Magento. The following diagram illustrates the structure of how this would be created using Magento websites, stores, and store views:

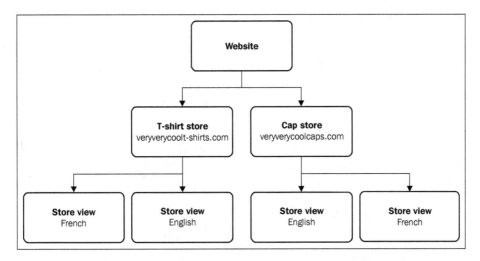

You can chose whether the stores share the customer data or whether each store has its own customer data, requiring customers to register separately if they want to order from both the t-shirt store and cap store.

# Using multiple store views in Magento

You can make use of multiple store views in Magento to customize how a store is presented; this is typically used to present the same store in multiple languages. In the following diagram, both stores have a French and English version, created at the Magento store view level:

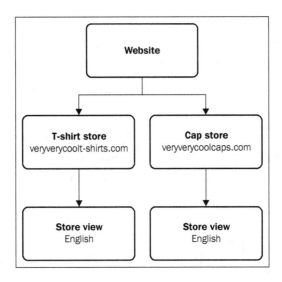

Magento allows the following two types of themes:

- A parent theme that contains all the files that are required to be run by Magento
- A child theme contains one or more files. Where a file isn't overwritten; Magento will look for the file in the parent theme

A parent theme is useful when you want to create a highly customized Magento theme from the standard themes that Magento has installed. Child themes are of use when you only want to make fairly minor amendments to your theme.

# Magento theme files

As you have already seen, Magento themes use a number of different types of files to change how your e-commerce website is displayed to your customers. The following four groups of files are associated with Magento themes:

- Skin files
- Layout files
- Template files
- Locale files

# Skin files

Skins encompass the files that you would associate with a website's design: the CSS, images, and JavaScript your theme requires in order to display your store.

In Magento, skin files are located in the `/skin/frontend/` directory. Magento's base skin files are stored in the `/skin/frontend/base/default` directory of your Magento installation, while theme files, which you would typically edit for custom themes that you create, would be included in the `/skin/frontend/name-of-your-package/name-of-your-theme/` directory.

In the examples used in this book, you will be building a theme in the default package, so your skin directory will look like this: `/skin/frontend/default/name-of-your-theme/`.

# Layout files

Magento uses XML layout files in its themes to inform Magento about which blocks are displayed where in the page and in what order, for example, the **MY CART** and **COMPARE PRODUCTS** widgets that use Magento's default theme, as shown in the following screenshot:

The Magento layout can also be used to add and remove CSS and JavaScript files as well as other elements from the `<head>` element of your Magento theme and alter the order and location of the links.

Magento's base layout files are stored in the `/app/design/frontend/base/default/layout` directory of your Magento installation, while your custom theme's layout files can be found in the `/app/design/frontend/name-of-your-package/name-of-your-theme/layout` directory.

In the examples used in this book, you will be building a theme in the default package, so your application directory will look like this: `/app/design/frontend/default/name-of-your-theme/`.

# Template files

Magento's template files (which use the `.phtml` file extension to indicate a mixture of PHP and HTML) provide your Magento theme with a way to generate the HTML for your store's pages using the data and content stored within Magento.

Magento's base template files are stored in the `/app/design/frontend/base/default/template` directory of your Magento installation, while your custom theme's layout files would be found in the `/app/design/frontend/default/name-of-your-theme/template` directory.

# Locale files

Finally, Magento's locale files help you customize the text in the interface elements of your Magento store, such as the text used as links in the userbar for your store, as shown in the following screenshot:

A Magento locale file can also be used to provide a translation of your store's elements to French, or even just American English to British English. In the preceding example, a locale file might change the **My Cart** link to **My Basket**, for instance.

The content of pages and products of your store can be translated by creating new products and pages in your new store's language within the store view for that particular language.

Magento locale files are stored in the `/app/design/frontend/base/default/locale` directory, with locale files specific to your theme being stored in the `/app/design/frontend/name-of-your-package/name-of-your-theme/locale` directory. Translations are stored in a `translate.csv` file; for example, `/app/design/frontend/default/name-of-your-theme/locale/en_GB/translate.csv` contains the translations for British English for that particular theme.

# Packages

In Magento theming, a package typically encapsulates a default theme that contains all of the skin, template, layout, and locale files Magento needs to render the website. It might also contain another non-default theme that customizes the look and feel of the website on top of the base theme, as illustrated in the following diagram:

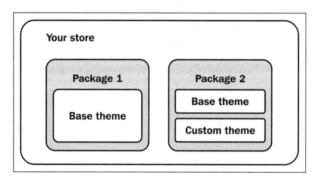

Assigning a package at the website level means that all the stores under that store level inherit that package. This would simply apply the theme to all of the stores assigned to that particular website in Magento. So, by assigning a theme at the website level in the following diagram, the **Cap store** and the **T-shirt store** would inherit the same theme, unless it was specifically overwritten at the individual store view level:

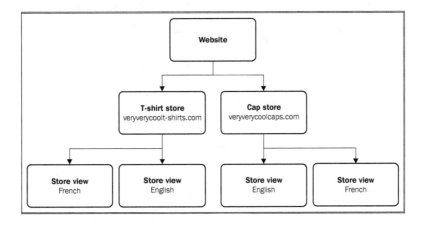

# Magento theme hierarchy

Magento has a hierarchy in place for its themes, which tells the system where to look for files if multiple themes are active on different stores on your website. As an example, think about a simple Magento store setup like the one you saw earlier, as demonstrated in the following diagram:

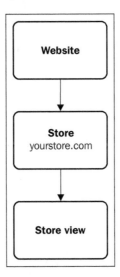

Now, imagine that your store has a theme called newtheme installed at the store view level. The Magento theme here requests a file called styles.css in the most specific interface and package first, so if you have a custom theme enabled, Magento will look in /skin/frontend/default/newtheme first. If it's not found in these directories, Magento looks in the default interfaces next: /app/design/frontend/ /default/default or /skin/frontend/default/default. Next, Magento will look in the base directories: /app/design/frontend/base/default or /skin/ frontend/base/default. If the specified file is not found after that, Magento will encounter a rendering error.

So, the deeper down the hierarchy tree of themes the file is, the more specific it is and the more precedence it takes over other more general files.

# Summary

This chapter provided you with an introduction to both Magento and Magento's themes as well as giving you an overview of what already exists in terms of the themes that ship with Magento by default. You have seen what comprises a Magento theme, some of the existing themes available with Magento 1.8, common theme terminology used in Magento, and how the Magento theme hierarchy works.

# Magento Theming Basics 2

Now that you've been introduced to the concepts behind Magento and Magento themes, the real work begins. This chapter covers the basics of getting up and running with a new Magento theme. This includes:

- Creating a new Magento theme
- Enabling the theme on your Magento store
- Changing your store's logo
- Changing the theme's favorites icon
- Customizing Magento's product watermark images
- Customizing Magento's product placeholder images
- Developer tools: Template Path Hints

## Creating a new Magento theme

As you saw in *Chapter 1, Introduction to Magento and Magento Themes*, a Magento theme can encompass very few files or a large number of files.

Firstly, create the new directories in your Magento installation to contain your new theme's files:

- `app/design/frontend/default/m18/template`
- `app/design/frontend/default/m18/layout`
- `app/design/frontend/default/m18/locale`
- `app/design/frontend/default/m18/etc`
- `skin/frontend/default/m18/css`
- `skin/frontend/default/m18/images`
- `skin/frontend/default/m18/js`

Once you have created these directories, you can create a file called `styles.css` in the `skin/frontend/default/m18/css` directory. To be able to test that your new skin is enabled, add the following to your `styles.css` file:

```
body {
background: red;
}
```

**Downloading the example code**

You can download the example code files for all Packt books you have purchased from your account at `http://www.packtpub.com`. If you purchased this book elsewhere, you can visit `http://www.packtpub.com/support` and register to have the files e-mailed directly to you.

Your next step is to enable your newly created Magento theme!

# Enabling a Magento theme

Now that you have the bare bones of your new Magento theme ready, you can enable your Magento theme. Log in to your Magento store's administration panel and navigate to the **System | Configuration** menu, as shown in the following screenshot:

Magento's administration panel is located at `example.com/admin` if you have installed Magento at `example.com`.

Once there, select the **Design** tab that has appeared in the left-hand column of the screen, keeping the **Current Configuration Scope** drop-down menu's value set to **Default Config**:

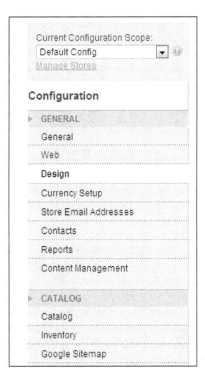

Next, expand the **Themes** section of the **Design** settings panel and enter the name of your Magento theme for the **Default** field here. In the following example, m18 is used as the name of the new Magento theme you are enabling:

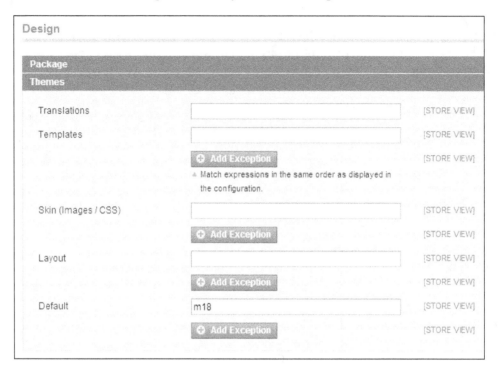

Once you have done this, you need to click on the **Save Config** button in the top-right of the screen, after which you will see the **The configuration has been saved** success message, as shown in the following screenshot:

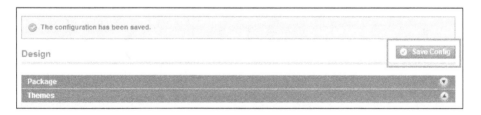

That's it! Your new Magento theme has been enabled. To test this, visit the frontend customer-facing side of your Magento store and refresh the page. You should be able see that the `styles.css` file removes all of the styles from the previously enabled theme and presents you with a rather unattractive screen, as shown in the following screenshot:

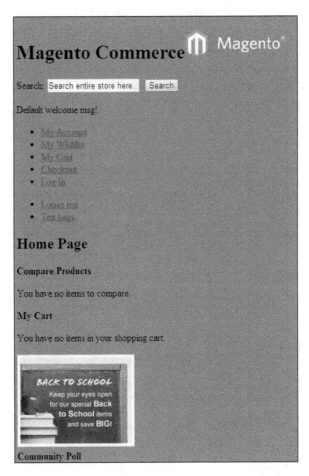

You can remove the `styles.css` file for now to return to Magento default theme styling; we will come back to customizing your theme's CSS in the later chapters.

# Changing your Magento store's logo

The next task you will perform in order to customize your Magento store's look and feel is to change your Magento theme's logo. Firstly, you will need to upload your store's logo file to your store, in the `/skin/frontend/default/m18/images` directory of your Magento installation.

Now, log in to your Magento store's administration panel and navigate to **System | Configuration**, and then to the **Design** tab. Expand the **Header** panel as shown in the following screenshot, and enter the value of your logo file's name and your theme's image directory. In this case, the example uses `images/logo.png` because the theme's logo file is stored at `/skin/frontend/default/m18/images/logo.png`.

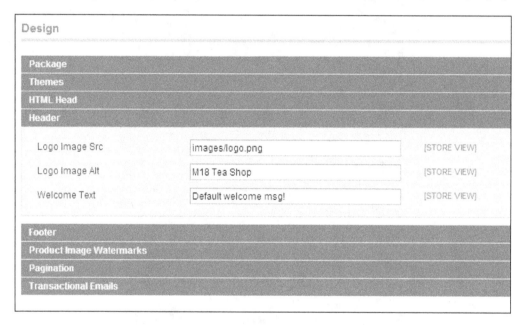

Click on the **Save Config** button in the top-right corner of the screen to save these changes. After refreshing your store, your new logo should appear in place of the default Magento logo:

 If you haven't created your own categories in your store yet, you may see Magento's sample category data appear in this menu or no categories at all. To add categories to your store, navigate to **Catalog** | **Manage Categories** in your Magento store's control panel.

# Customizing your store's favorites icon (favicon)

Alongside your logo, you can use your store's favorites icon (**favicon**) to help distinguish yourself from other websites. The favicon is typically displayed in your browser's address bar and tabs, as seen in the following screenshot in the top-left of the screenshot:

To change your store's favicon from the default Magento favicon, you will need to create a `favicon.ico` file.

 You can create `favicon.ico` files using free online tools such as the one at `http://tools.dynamicdrive.com/favicon/`.

Once you have your `favicon.ico` file ready, upload it to your Magento installation's `/skin/frontend/design/default/your-theme-name/` directory. In the example theme, this would be `/skin/frontend/default/m18/`. You will now be able to see your custom favicon appear for your store, as shown in the following screenshot:

 It's also worth checking the guide on adding home icons and other mobile and handheld-device specific icons to your Magento theme, covered in *Chapter 7, Magento Theming for Mobile and Tablet Devices*.

# Customizing Magento's product watermark image

Some stores like to watermark their images to promote brand consistency across their websites, or to protect their product photography from being used without permission on other websites.

Magento allows you to specify a watermark image to overlay product photographs in your store. To change this, you can navigate to **System | Configuration** in your Magento store's administration panel. From there, navigate to the **Design** tab on the left-hand side, and then expand the **Product Image Watermarks** panel, as shown in the following screenshot:

| **Product Image Watermarks** | | |
|---|---|---|
| Base Image Watermark Default Size | | [STORE VIEW] |
| | Example format: 200x300. | |
| Base Image Watermark Opacity, Percent | | [STORE VIEW] |
| Base Image Watermark | Choose File   No file chosen | [STORE VIEW] |
| | Allowed file types: jpeg, gif, png. | |
| Base Image Watermark Position | Stretch ▾ | [STORE VIEW] |
| Small Image Watermark Default Size | | [STORE VIEW] |
| | Example format: 200x300. | |
| Small Image Watermark Opacity, Percent | | [STORE VIEW] |
| Small Image Watermark | Choose File   No file chosen | [STORE VIEW] |
| | Allowed file types: jpeg, gif, png. | |
| Small Image Watermark Position | Stretch ▾ | [STORE VIEW] |
| Thumbnail Watermark Default Size | | [STORE VIEW] |
| | Example format: 200x300. | |
| Thumbnail Watermark Opacity, Percent | | [STORE VIEW] |
| Thumbnail Watermark | Choose File   No file chosen | [STORE VIEW] |
| | Allowed file types: jpeg, gif, png. | |
| Thumbnail Watermark Position | Stretch ▾ | [STORE VIEW] |

Firstly, upload a watermark image you wish to be displayed across product images using the **Base Image Watermark** field, and click on the **Save Config** button in the top-right corner of your screen. If you now view a product on your Magento store front, you will see the product image appear with the watermark image superimposed over it. It's wise to make the watermark as faint as you can and try to position it in a way that does not obscure the product photography, unlike the following example:

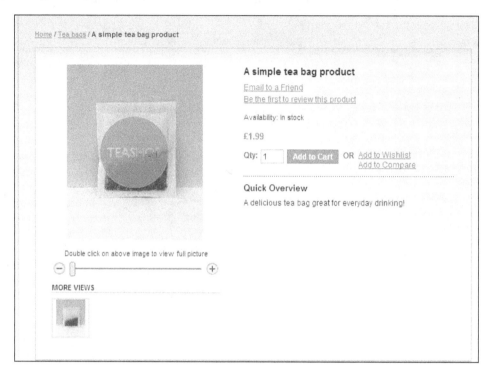

>  You may need to refresh Magento's image cache before you see the watermark appear over your images. Navigate to **System | Cache Management**, and click on the **Flush Catalog Images Cache** button towards the bottom of this screen to regenerate the product images with the watermark over them.

# Using product images in Magento

By default, the three product image types in Magento are used in different templates and areas of your Magento site:

- **Thumbnail images**: These are used in the image gallery (if you have more than one image displayed on a product page), the cart, and the default **Related Products** block displayed in Magento's sidebar (50 x 50 pixels on the default theme)

- **Small images**: These are used in product listings on category pages, in cross-sell and up-sell blocks, and search result pages (135 x 135 pixels on the default theme)

- **Base images**: These are used on Magento product pages and the product image zoom feature, if the image is large enough (262 x 262 pixels on the default theme)

The **Product Image Watermarks** panel allows you to specify separate watermark images to appear on your **Base Image**, **Small Image**, and **Thumbnail** images. You can change how and where the watermark image appears over the product photograph by making use of the **Position** field dropdowns. In particular:

- The **Stretch** option stretches the watermark image across the full product image height and width, which can look blurry if your watermark image is too small

- The **Center** option centers the image both vertically and horizontally over the product photograph

- The **Tile** option repeats the placeholder image over the image, assuming the placeholder image is small enough to be able to be repeated over the product photograph

- The remaining images tell Magento where to place the watermark image over the product photograph

The **Default Size** field allows you to specify the size of the watermark image as applied to the product image; this value is in pixels, in the form of width x height for example, 200 x 350 would resize the placeholder image to a width of 200 pixels and a height of 350 pixels.

Finally, the **Opacity** field allows you to set the opacity of each of the product watermark images as a percentage. A value of `100` in these fields would cause the watermark to be fully visible, and obscure the product photograph fully or partially Lower values will show a semi-transparent watermark image over the product photographs, while `0` will not display the watermark image at all.

[ The `watermark.png` file is included in your book's code files. ]

# Customizing Magento's product placeholder images

In addition to the product watermarks that can be laid over product images, Magento allows you to customize the default image placeholder image, which is used when a product has no product image available to be displayed.

To see the default Magento image placeholder, you can create a product and simply not assign it an image, which will result in something similar to the result in the following screenshot:

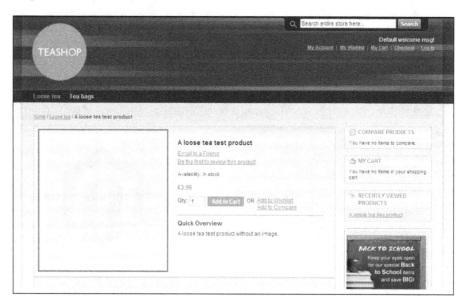

You can add products to your website by navigating to **Catalog | Manage Products** in your Magento store's administration panel.

 As most e-commerce store owners will testify, it's best to include product imagery on product pages, but there may be occasions where you might like to sell products through your store and may not have an image immediately available, so this is a good way to reinforce your store's brand!

To customize your store's product placeholder images, navigate to **System | Configuration** in your Magento store's administration panel and select the **Catalog** option from the left-hand menu. From there, expand the **Product Image Placeholders** panel, as shown in the following screenshot:

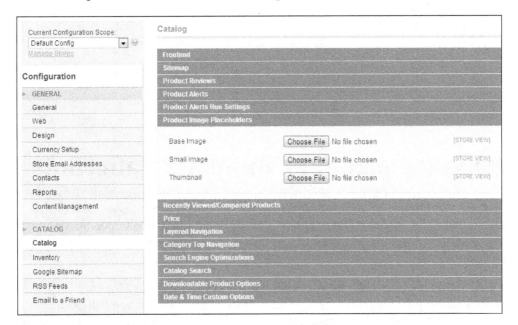

You can upload your custom product photograph placeholders here, using the **Base Image**, **Small Image**, and **Thumbnail** fields. These replace the placeholder image in the various sizes used throughout your Magento store, enabling you to define separate images for each occasion.

Once you have uploaded your new product placeholder images, click on the **Save Config** button at the top-right side of the screen to save your changes, and go back and refresh the page of your product without an image assigned:

# Using the Magento Template Path Hints

As you might expect from a powerful e-commerce system such as Magento, there are tools to help make your job as a Magento theme developer easier. One of the most useful tools for theme developers is **Template Path Hints**, which tells you where each block's template in your Magento store's page is stored in your Magento theme directories.

To enable this tool, navigate to **System | Configuration** in your Magento administration panel and change the **Current Configuration Scope** field's value to your store view's value. In the example in the following screenshot, you can see this being set to **Default Store View**:

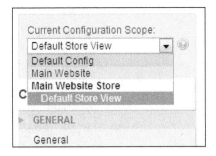

Now, select the **Developer** tab towards the bottom of the list grouped under **ADVANCED**:

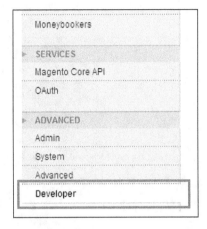

Expand the **Debug** panel and you are now presented with a selection of options; set the value for the **Template Path Hints** field to **Yes**, as seen in the following screenshot (you may need to uncheck the **Use Website** checkbox before you can do this):

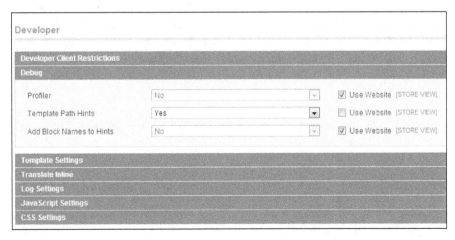

For more advanced template hints on Magento theming, see the module available at `http://www.fabrizio-branca.de/magento-advanced-template-hints-20.html`.

Finally, click on the **Save Config** button to save these changes, and refresh one of the pages on the frontend of your Magento store to see the tool appear.

You may need to refresh your Magento's store caches to see these appear. To clear your cache, navigate to **System | Cache Management** and clear the **Blocks HTML output** cache. You can also fully disable all the caches from this menu, which is beneficial for theme development!

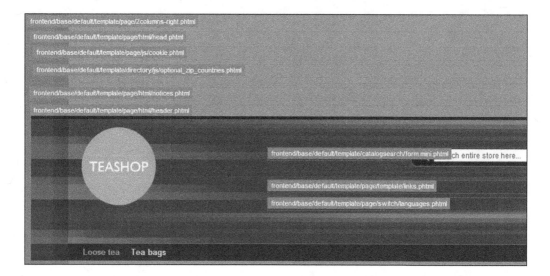

It is possible to restrict these hints' display to specific IP addresses too, by expanding the **Developer Client Restrictions** panel above the **Debug** panel and entering your IP address in the **Allowed IPs (comma separated)** field:

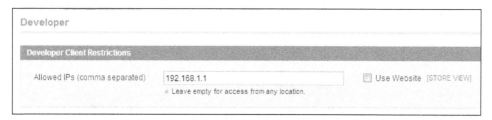

Only visitors using the IP address(es) specified in this field will see the debug tools you have enabled once you save this configuration.

# Summary

This chapter introduced the beginnings of customizing your Magento store's look and feel, including how to create a new Magento theme, enabling your new Magento theme, as well as changing your store's logo and favicon, customizing Magento's product watermark images and Magento's product placeholder images, and exploring Magento's Template Path Hints tool to help you better understand where Magento is requesting template files from.

Future chapters dive deeper into specific areas of Magento theme development.

# 3
# Magento Templates

So far, the changes to your Magento theme have been fairly simple and largely limited to configuration within Magento itself. This chapter looks more deeply at customizing templates within your Magento theme to start making more complex changes to your Magento store's look and feel. In this chapter, we will cover the following topics:

- Providing some simple layout styles for your Magento theme
- Customizing your store's header
- Customizing the search box
- Adding a static block to a template
- Customizing your store's footer
- Customizing your store's checkout and cart

## Providing layout style for your Magento theme

The first thing you can provide for your Magento theme is some basic CSS to define the column's width and layout. Before you do this, you can use a simple CSS reset to remove unnecessary margins and padding from the elements:

```
* {
margin:0;
padding:0;
}
img {
border:0;
vertical-align:top;
}
```

```
a {
color:#1e7ec8;
text-decoration:underline;
}
a:hover        {
text-decoration:none;
}
:focus {
outline:0;
}
```

 An alternative to CSS resets is `normalize.css`, which you can download from `http://necolas.github.io/ normalize.css/`.

To do this, you can make use of what is provided in Magento's Default theme. Open the `styles.css` file in the `/skin/frontend/default/default/css/` directory and you will see a block of CSS that begins:

```
/* Layout ======================================================
==================== */
.wrapper {
min-width:954px;
}
.page-print {
background:#fff;
padding:25px 30px;
text-align:left;
}
.page-empty {
background:#fff;
padding:20px;
text-align:left;
}
.page-popup {
background:#fff;
padding:25px 30px;
text-align:left;
}
.main-container {
background:#fbfaf6 url(../images/bkg_main1.gif) 50% 0 no-repeat;
}
```

```
.main {
background:#fffffe url(../images/bkg_main2.gif) 0 0 no-repeat;
margin:0 auto;
min-height:400px;
padding:25px 25px 80px;
text-align:left;
width:900px;
}
```

Copy this into your own theme's `styles.css` file, in the `/skin/frontend/default/ m18/css/` directory you previously created, and adapt it to remove any mention of the default theme's color and images:

```
.wrapper {
min-width:954px;
}
.page-print {
background:#fff;
padding:25px 30px;
text-align:left;
}
.page-empty {
background:#fff;
padding:20px;
text-align:left;
}
.page-popup {
background:#fff;
padding:25px 30px;
text-align:left;
}
.main-container {
background:#f6f6f6;
}
.main {
background:#fff;
color: #333;
margin:0 auto;
min-height:400px;
padding:25px 25px 80px;
text-align:left;
width:900px;
}
```

Magento themes typically provide three different page layouts to be used: one-column, two-column, and three-column templates. The next block of CSS you can copy from the `/skin/frontend/default/default/css/styles.css` file is the CSS that defines the width and position for each of these layouts:

```css
.col-left {
float:left;
padding:0 0 1px;
width:195px
}
.col-main {
float:left;
padding:0 0 1px;
width:685px
}
.col-right {
float:right;
padding:0 0 1px;
width:195px
}
.col1-layout .col-main {
float:none;
width:auto
}
.col3-layout .col-main {
margin-left:17px;
width:475px
}
.col3-layout .col-wrapper {
float:left;
width:687px
}
.col2-set .col-1 {
float:left;
width:48.5%
}
.col2-set .col-2 {
float:right;
width:48.5%
}
.col2-set .col-narrow {
width:32%
}
```

```
.col2-set .col-wide {
width:65%
}
.col3-set .col-1 {
float:left;
width:32%
}
.col3-set .col-2 {
float:left;
margin-left:2%;
width:32%
}
.col3-set .col-3 {
float:right;
width:32%
}
.col4-set .col-2 {
float:left;
margin:0 2%;
width:23.5%
}
.col4-set .col-4 {
float:right;
width:23.5%
}
.col2-left-layout .col-main,.col3-layout .col-wrapper .col-main {
float:right
}
.col4-set .col-1,.col4-set .col-3 {
float:left;
width:23.5%
}
```

The preceding CSS alters the width of the columns based on which particular layout is in use, for example, if a page is using a three-column layout, the column widths are adapted so that all three columns can be contained within one row of your page, rather than displaying them above and below each other.

Next, you will need to specify an additional layout for the header and footer areas of your theme:

```
.header-container, .footer-container {
background: #f6f6f6;
}
```

```
.header, .footer {
margin: 0 auto;
width: 930px
}
```

Finally, to complete the layout, you will need to include CSS to clear the floating elements used in your layout, again taken from the bottom of the `styles.css` file in the `/skin/frontend/default/default/css/` folder and copied into the bottom of your `styles.css` file in the `/skin/frontend/default/m18/css/` folder.

 You can find this in the code files for this chapter.

If you now refresh your Magento store's frontend, you will see the effect this CSS has had, overwriting the default theme's previous styling, but retaining the column layout of the store as you can see in the following screenshot:

As you can see, this provides a basic starting point for your custom Magento theme, but there's still much work to be done!

# Customizing your Magento store's header

As it stands, your current theme looks incomplete at the moment. You can begin to address this by:

- Adding CSS to customize the header elements of your theme
- Altering your theme's `header.phtml` file to customize the HTML used by Magento

## Providing CSS for Magento's navigation dropdowns

Most of the styling for Magento's drop-down navigation can be done within CSS. Firstly, you can remove the bullet points and other styling associated with the `<ul>` elements by adding the following CSS:

```
.links li, #nav li, .breadcrumbs li {
display: inline;
list-style: none;
}
ul.links, .links li, .breadcrumbs ul, #nav ul {
margin: 0;
padding: 0;
}
```

Our next task is to restore your Magento theme's CSS for drop-down navigation . This can be done by reusing the CSS applied to `#nav` from the `styles.css` file in the `/skin/frontend/default/default/css/` folder and copying this into your new theme's `styles.css` file in the `/skin/frontend/default/default/css/` folder, updating the color references as you wish.

 You can see this CSS in your code sample file in the chapter's `skin\css` folder provided with this book.

This will provide basic styling for your Magento store's navigation structure as you can see in the following screenshot:

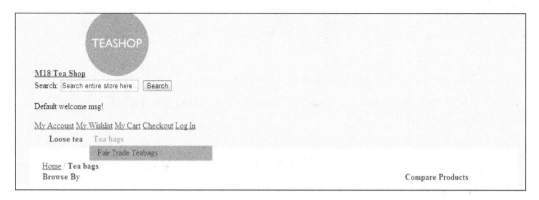

# Altering the header.phtml template

As you saw, when you enabled Magento's **Template Path Hints** tool, the pages on your Magento store were composed from many different templates. The header and footer, which are generally used globally throughout your store, are added to the top and bottom of each page respectively, while different page structures (for example, one-column, two-column, and three-column layouts) are swapped in and out as defined by the Magento layout, either by a theme or at a page level through Magento's CMS tool.

 To see which template is being used, you can enable Magento's Template Path Hints file. See *Chapter 2, Magento Theming Basics*, for a walkthrough of how to do this.

Now, view your Magento store's frontend and you can see the extent of your Magento theme's header file within the design:

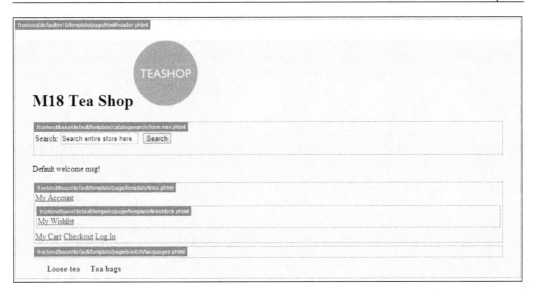

To change the markup in your Magento theme's header, copy the `header.phtml` file in the `/app/design/frontend/base/default/template/page/html/` directory to the `/app/design/frontend/default/m18/template/page/html/` directory. You can provide a typical layout for your store's header in line with the following diagram:

The first thing you need to do is alter how the logo is displayed to remove the text alongside it. Open the `header.phtml` file in your theme and find the following block of code:

```php
<?php if ($this->getIsHomePage()):?>
<h1 class="logo"><strong><?php echo $this->getLogoAlt() ?></
strong><a href="<?php echo $this->getUrl('') ?>" title="<?php echo
$this->getLogoAlt() ?>" class="logo"><img src="<?php echo $this-
>getLogoSrc() ?>" alt="<?php echo $this->getLogoAlt() ?>" /></a></h1>
<?php else:?>
<a href="<?php echo $this->getUrl('') ?>" title="<?php echo $this-
>getLogoAlt() ?>" class="logo"><strong><?php echo $this->getLogoAlt()
?></strong><img src="<?php echo $this->getLogoSrc() ?>" alt="<?php
echo $this->getLogoAlt() ?>" /></a>
<?php endif?>
```

This is currently adding text to the logo block on both, the homepage (wrapped in a `<h1>` element on the homepage using the `$this->getIsHomePage()` function to check whether the current page is the homepage) and other pages (wrapped in a `<strong>` element). The logo file is specified in the Magento configuration, which was covered in *Chapter 2, Magento Theming Basics*. Update this to reflect the following code, to output the logo's image simply:

```
<a href="<?php echo $this->getUrl('') ?>" title="<?php echo
$this->getLogoAlt() ?>" class="logo"><img src="<?php echo $this-
>getLogoSrc() ?>" alt="<?php echo $this->getLogoAlt() ?>" /></a>
```

Once saved, refresh your Magento site and you will see that the change has been applied:

Next, you will need to apply some CSS in your theme's `styles.css` file to improve the layout of the header's elements:

```
.header .logo, .header .quick-access {
float: left;
margin: 1%;
width: 48%;
}
.header .quick-access {
text-align: right;
}
```

If you refresh your store after saving these changes, you will see that the header now looks more like what you would expect:

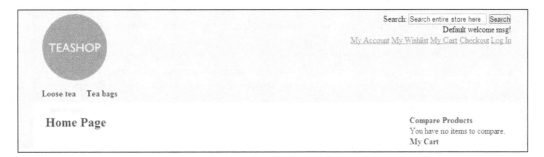

# Customizing Magento's search box

You can also customize Magento's search feature through the Magento templates. The search feature is especially important for stores with a large number of products, so ensuring that it is in a prominent place and looks like a search feature is very important.

Firstly, to overwrite the template used for the search form in the header, copy the `search.mini.phtml` file at `/app/design/frontend/base/default/template/catalogsearch/` into the `/app/design/frontend/default/m18/template/catalogsearch` directory, and find the following lines that constitute the **Search** button:

```
<button type="submit" title="<?php echo $this->__('Search') ?>" class="button">
<span><span>
<?php echo $this->__('Search') ?>
</span></span>
</button>
```

Remove the `<span>` elements highlighted in the preceding code, as these are no longer required in the new theme. Open your theme's `styles.css` file to provide some basic styling for the search text box and change its border color when it is focused on the following:

```
.input-text {
border: 1px #CCC solid;
border-radius: 3px;
padding: 3px;
}
  .input-text:active, .input-text:focus {
  border-color: #e57d04;
  }
```

Removing the `<span>` elements helps to reduce the weight of the pages provided to customers a little, increasing the loading time of your store. However, if you aren't planning to heavily customize your Magento theme, you can leave these as they appear quite frequently throughout many Magento templates and can take some weeding out!

Next, you can add some styling to the buttons throughout your theme:

```
.button {
background: #e57d04;
border: none;
border-radius: 3px;
color: #fff;
font-weight: bold;
padding: 3px;
text-align: center;
}
.button:active, .button:focus {
background-color: #333;
}
```

Finally, you can add some styling to the search button specifically to include an image that will help your customers identify its purpose more easily:

```
.form-search .button {
background-image: url("../images/search.png");
background-repeat: no-repeat;
background-position: 3px center;
padding-left: 24px;
}
```

If you now refresh your Magento theme, you will see the change take effect:

# Adding a static block to a Magento template

Sometimes, you may need to add an editable block to your template to allow content to be easily updated through Magento's administration panel. Magento's static blocks allow you to do this, and they can be embedded in the Magento templates.

## Creating a new static block

Firstly, you will need to create a static block in Magento. Log in to your store's administration panel and navigate to **CMS | Static Blocks**, as shown in the following screenshot:

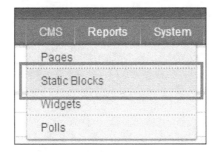

Here, click on the **Add New Block** button at the top-right of your screen, as shown in the following screenshot:

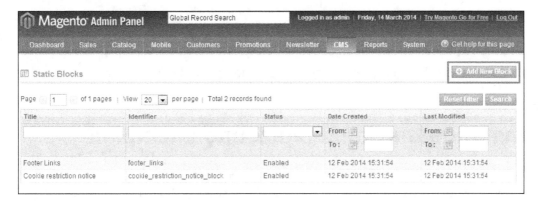

You can create your block here: the block **Title** field allows you to give your block a name, while the **Identifier** field is a machine-readable way to identify this specific block (remember this value, as you'll need it soon!).

 Note that the value of the **Identifier** field cannot contain spaces or special characters, and it's typical to use an underscore character (_) here to separate words in the identifier's name.

The **Status** field allows you to enable or disable this specific block: ensure this is set to **Enabled** to be able to make use of the block in your template. Finally, the **Content** field allows you to specify content for this block; you can either make use of the Magento text editor tool here, or disable it and enter raw HTML. The following screenshot shows an example block:

Once you're ready, click on the **Save Block** button towards the top-right corner of your screen.

# Inserting the static block into a template

Now that you have a static block ready, you can include it in a template within your Magento theme. The example static block created previously is for use in the footer of the website to give customers an idea what the store is about.

Before you do this, you will need to copy the `footer.phtml` file from the `/app/design/frontend/base/default/template/page/html/` directory to the `/app/design/frontend/default/m18/page/html/` directory and locate the following lines:

```
<div class="footer-container">
<div class="footer">
```

Below these lines, insert the following snippet to insert the static block you created into the page at this point:

```
<div class="footer-container">
<div class="footer">
<div class="footer-about footer-col">
<?php echo $this->getLayout()->createBlock('cms/block')-
>setBlockId('footer_about')->toHtml(); ?>
</div>
```

In the section that reads `setBlockId('footer_about')`, note that the `footer_about` value is the identifier value of the block you created earlier. In the preceding code, the `echo $this->getLayout()->createBlock('cms/block')->setBlockId('footer_about')->toHtml()` code tells Magento to insert the contents of the static block into Magento with the identifier `footer_about`.

If you refresh your Magento theme, you will see the new block's content appear in the footer area of your store:

TEASHOP is an online emporium of the finest tea.
* About Us
* Customer Service
* Privacy Policy
Site Map Search Terms Advanced Search Orders and Returns Contact Us
Help Us to Keep Magento Healthy - Report All Bugs (ver. 1.8.1.0)
© 2013 Magento Demo Store. All Rights Reserved.

# Customizing your Magento store's footer

Your theme's footer is currently quite unstyled and contains a lot of links you may not require. Open your theme's `footer.phtml` file in the `/app/design/frontend/default/m18/template/page/html/` directory and you will see something similar to the following code:

```
<div class="footer-container">
    <div class="footer">
      <div class="footer-about footer-col">
        <?php echo $this->getLayout()->createBlock('cms/block')-
>setBlockId('footer_about')->toHtml(); ?>
      </div>
        <?php echo $this->getChildHtml() ?>
        <p class="bugs"><?php echo $this->__('Help Us to Keep Magento
Healthy') ?> - <a href="http://www.magentocommerce.com/bug-tracking"
onclick="this.target='_blank'"><strong><?php echo $this->__('Report
All Bugs') ?></strong></a> <?php echo $this->__('(ver. %s)',
Mage::getVersion()) ?></p>
        <address><?php echo $this->getCopyright() ?></address>
    </div>
</div>
```

By removing the preceding highlighted code, you can begin to clean up your theme's footer and customize it for your own store. You can gain a little more control over the footer's layout by adding an additional `<div>` element around the content, as highlighted in the following code:

```
<div class="footer-container">
    <div class="footer">
      <div class="footer-about footer-col">
        <?php echo $this->getLayout()->createBlock('cms/block')-
>setBlockId('footer_about')->toHtml(); ?>
      </div>
<div class="footer-col footer-categories">
        <?php echo $this->getChildHtml() ?>
  </div>
        <address><?php echo $this->getCopyright() ?></address>
    </div>
</div>
```

You can now add some CSS to your theme's `styles.css` file to help provide a clearer layout for the content in the footer:

```
.footer-col {
float: left;
```

```
margin: 1%;
width: 48%;
}
.footer address {
clear: both;
text-align: center;
}
.footer ul {
list-style: none;
}
    .footer ul li {
    display: block;
    }
.footer a {
color: #333;
text-decoration: none;
}
    .footer a:active, .footer a:hover {
    text-decoration: underline;
    }
```

You can also add some styling for specific content blocks in the footer you
have created:

```
.footer-about p:first-of-type {
color: #e57d04;
font-size: 135%;
}
.footer-categories {
text-align: right;
}
```

If you now look at your theme's footer, you will see that it looks much more fitting
for a Magento store:

TEASHOP is an online emporium of the finest tea.

About Us
Customer Service
Privacy Policy
Site Map
Search Terms
Advanced Search
Orders and Returns
Contact Us

© 2013 Magento Demo Store. All Rights Reserved.

# Listing all top-level categories in your Magento store

Many stores include a list of their top-level (primary) categories in their footer to help customers navigate to their products more easily. You can do this by adding a simple snippet of code to the footer template you have already customized. Open your theme's `footer.phtml` file and add the following highlighted code:

```
<div class="footer-container">
    <div class="footer">
      <div class="footer-about footer-col">
        <?php echo $this->getLayout()->createBlock('cms/block')-
>setBlockId('footer_about')->toHtml(); ?>
        <?php
            $_helper = Mage::helper('catalog/category');
            $_categories = $_helper->getStoreCategories();
            if (count($_categories) > 0): ?>
                <ul>
                    <?php foreach($_categories as $_category): ?>
                    <li><a href="<?php echo $_helper-
>getCategoryUrl($_category) ?>"><?php echo $_category->getName() ?>
</a></li>
                    <?php endforeach; ?>
                </ul>
            <?php endif; ?>
      </div>
      <div class="footer-col footer-categories">
        <?php echo $this->getChildHtml() ?>
      </div>
      <address><?php echo $this->getCopyright() ?></address>
    </div>
</div>
```

 For more information on the Mage Helper class, see the Magento documentation at `http://docs.magentocommerce.com/ Mage_Core/Mage_Core_Helper_Abstract.html`.

Once you have saved this change, you should see your top-level categories appear in the footer:

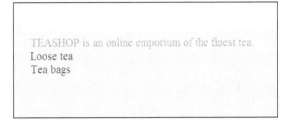

# Customizing your store's checkout and cart

You can pay some attention to the styling of your store's checkout and cart templates to better match the feel of your new Magento theme.

## Styling the cart page

To view the cart page as it currently appears, add a product from your store to the cart and use the **My Cart** button in the header of your website:

Open your theme's `styles.css` file in the `/skin/frontend/default/m18/css/`
directory and add the following CSS to the bottom of the file to style the cart table,
which contains the products your customer is about to buy:

```css
fieldset {
border: 0;
}
.a-right {
text-align: right;
}
.checkout-types, .form-list {
list-style: none;
margin: 10px 0;
}
.totals {
float: right;
}
.totals table {
width: 100%;
}
.checkout-types, .totals {
text-align: right;
}
.checkout-types li, .form-list li {
display: inline;
margin-right: 5px;
}
.form-list li.control {
display: block;
}
.data-table {
width: 100%;
}
.data-table a {
color: #000;
}
.data-table th, .data-table .even {
background: #f6f6f6;
}
.data-table th, .data-table td {
border-bottom: 1px #DDD solid;
padding: 5px;
}
```

```
.discount, .shipping {
background: #f6f6f6;
border-radius: 5px;
margin-bottom: 10px;
padding: 5px;
}
```

Once this CSS has been added, your store's cart page will look more in line with your new Magento theme:

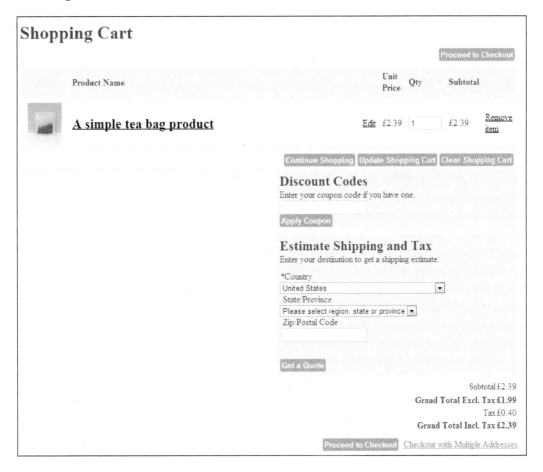

# Styling the checkout page

If you now click on the **Proceed to checkout** button on the cart screen, you will see Magento's checkout page, which currently looks similar to the following screenshot:

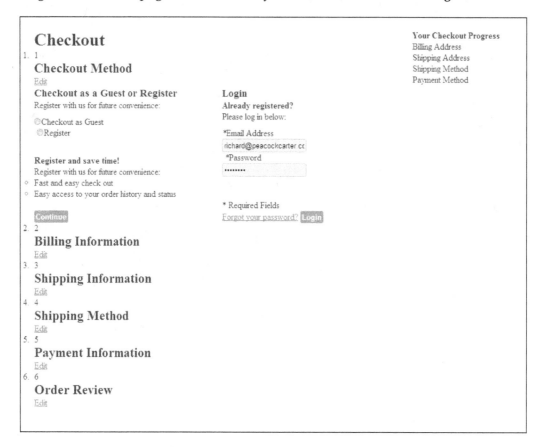

Add the following CSS to your theme's `styles.css` file to style the **Your Checkout Progress** block, which appears in the right-hand column of the checkout page to indicate to customers which stage of the checkout process they're at:

```
.block-progress {
border: 0;
margin: 0;
}
.block-progress dt {
background: #eee;
border: 1px solid #ccc;
color: #555;
```

```
font-size: 10px;
line-height: 1.35;
margin: 0 0 6px;
padding: 2px 8px;
text-transform: uppercase;
}
.block-progress dd {
border-top: 0;
padding: 2px 10px;
margin: 0 0 6px;
}
.block-progress dt.complete a {
text-transform: none;
}
.block-progress p {
margin: 0;
}
```

Next, adding the CSS below provides styling for the buttons and form elements within the one-page checkout:

```
.opc .buttons-set {
margin-top: 0;
padding-top: 2em;
}
.opc .buttons-set p.required {
margin: 0;
padding: 0 0 10px;
}
.opc .buttons-set.disabled button.button {
display: none;
}
.opc .buttons-set .please-wait {
height: 28px;
line-height: 28px;
}
.opc .ul {
list-style: disc outside;
padding-left: 18px;
}
```

Finally, adding the remaining CSS below provides the styling for the individual steps of the one-page checkout process, and different colors to indicate which particular step of the checkout your customer has completed:

```
.opc {
position: relative;
}
.opc .step-title {
background: #CCC;
border: 1px solid #CCC;
border-top-left-radius: 5px;
border-top-right-radius: 5px;
color: #555;
margin: 10px 0 0 0;
padding: 10px;
text-align: right;
}
.opc .step-title .number {
background: #fff;
border: 1px solid #fff;
border-radius: 3px;
color: #444;
float: left;
font: normal 11px/12px arial, helvetica, sans-serif;
margin: 0 5px 0 0;
padding: 0 3px;
}
.opc .step-title h2 {
color: #555;
float: left;
font: bold 12px/14px Arial, Helvetica, sans-serif;
margin: 0;
}
.opc .step-title a {
display: none;
float: right;
font-size: 11px;
line-height: 16px;
}
```

```
.opc .allow .step-title {
background: #999;
border-color: #999;
border-top-color: #fff;
color: #fff;
cursor: pointer;
}
.opc .allow .step-title h2 {
color: #fff;
}
.opc .allow .step-title a {
color: #fff;
display: block;
font-size: 10px;
text-transform: uppercase;
}
.opc .active .step-title {
background: #e57d04;
border: none;
color: #fff;
cursor: default;
}
.opc .active .step-title h2 {
color: #fff;
}
.opc .active .step-title a {
display: none;
}
.opc .step {
border: 1px solid #ccc;
border-top: 0;
background: #f9f9f9;
padding: 15px 30px;
position: relative;
}
.opc .step .tool-tip {
right: 30px;
}
```

If you now review your store's checkout, you will see that it is styled more neatly to help guide your customers through Magento's one-page checkout process:

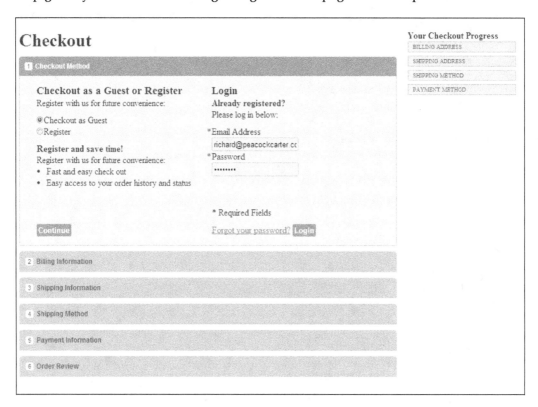

# Summary

This chapter explored how you can identify which Magento template is responsible for which block of content in your Magento theme. You also learned how you can use Magento template files to customize your theme, create a basic layout for your Magento theme, customize your store's header and the search feature, add a static block to a Magento template, customize your store's footer, and style your store's checkout and cart. Further chapters will dig deeper into ways to build your custom Magento theme using the Magento layout files and more advanced template manipulation.

# 4
# Magento Layout

You have now looked at the changes you can make to your Magento theme using CSS and template changes. This chapter introduces Magento's layout language, which can be used to change the appearance and order of blocks within your Magento theme and covers the following:

- Adding a `local.xml` file to your theme
- Changing the default page template
- Changing a page's layout via CMS
- Adding a static block to a page using the Magento layout
- Changing the ordering of blocks in Magento's sidebar
- Removing unnecessary blocks from Magento's sidebar
- Adding a new products block to your store's home page

## Adding local.xml to your Magento theme

As you have seen, Magento provides fallbacks to fill in the files not provided by your theme to help ensure your website functions as effectively as possible. You can overwrite the layout information in your Magento theme by applying a `local.xml` file to your Magento theme.

Create a file called `local.xml` in your theme's `/app/design/frontend/default/ m18/layout/` directory, and include the following XML:

```xml
<?xml version="1.0"?>
<layout>
</layout>
```

This is the very least your Magento XML layout file requires: all of the subsequent changes to your theme's layout need to be written in the `<layout>` element.

# Using layout to change your default Magento page template

Each page in your Magento store uses a skeleton layout; these are typically one of the following:

- One-column layout
- Two-column layout with a right-hand sidebar
- Two-column layout with a left-hand sidebar
- Three-column layout

Some pages may have specific templates assigned to them (for example, your one-page checkout may use the one-column layout while pages created through Magento's CMS tool may use a two-column layout with left sidebar layout), but pages that are not specifically given a layout inherit the default page layout.

## Types of blocks within Magento

There are two types of blocks within Magento:

- **Structural blocks**: These blocks provide regions that Magento can assign content blocks into. These structural blocks act as a skeleton for your store's content, and typically include the header, footer, content, and sidebar blocks.

- **Content blocks**: These blocks provide reusable blocks of content that are populated as required. Examples of content blocks in Magento include the category product listings (which would typically be included in the content structural block) and the category navigation block (typically assigned to the header structural block).

## Changing a page's template using the XML layout

You can change this default page layout in your Magento theme by adding Magento XML layout instructions in your theme's `local.xml` file. Open your theme's `local.xml` file you created in the previous section of this chapter, and add the following highlighted code to change the default page template to the one column layout:

```
<?xml version="1.0"?>
<layout>
  <default>
    <reference name="root">
```

```
    <action method="setTemplate">
      <template>page/1column.phtml</template>
    </action>
  </reference>
</default>
</layout>
```

The `<default>` handle applies this change to all, unless they are specifically overwritten for a particular type of page within Magento (for example, the one-page checkout or category pages), while the `<reference>` `name` attribute tells Magento where this change is to be made: the `<root>` applies this to the top-most structural block.

Finally, the `<action>` element in the XML tells Magento to use the template called `1column.phtml` in the `/page/` directory within your theme's templates directory.

> This path is relative to the `/app/design/frontend/default/m18/template/` directory if the file exists in the m18 theme, or else it will fallback and find this file in another default theme.

If you save this change, you will see that the one column layout is applied to pages without a more specific layout set through Magento's content management tool. On the example site, you can see that the **Orders & Returns** page (at `http://www.example.com/sales/guest/form/` if you installed Magento at `http://www.example.com`) has now adopted the one column layout you used in `local.xml` file:

Note that the product listings haven't been styled yet! You'll come to that later on.

# Changing a page's layout using Magento's CMS tool

Apart from using Magento layout files to define which pages use which page layouts, you can also use Magento's CMS to apply specific layouts to specific pages created through the content management tool.

 Layout changes specified in Magento's CMS tool will overwrite layout changes made within your theme's XML files.

The following example will edit the layout of the **About Us** page in the store, which has a two column including the right sidebar layout assigned to it by default, as you can see in the following screenshot:

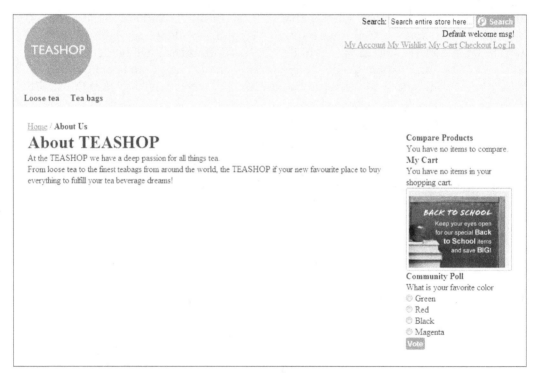

Log in to your Magento administration panel and navigate to **CMS** | **Pages**:

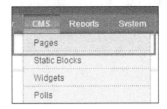

From here, select a page to edit by clicking on its corresponding row in the list of pages:

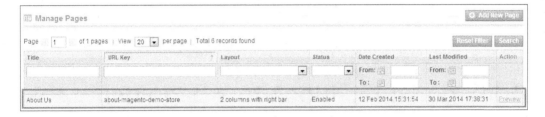

When editing the page you want to change the layout for, navigate to the Design tab that appears in the left-hand side column:

In the **Layout** field that appears under the **Page Layout** block, as shown in the following screenshot, you can select an available page layout from the dropdown. Select the **1 column** option and click on the **Save Page** button at the top-right corner of the screen to save this setting:

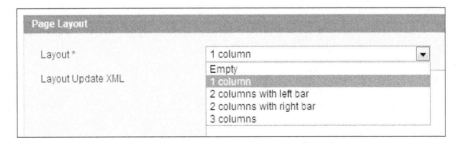

If you now view the frontend of your Magento store and navigate to the **About Us** page you edited, you will see that the new layout has been applied:

# Adding a static block to a page using the Magento layout

As you saw in the previous chapter on Magento templates, you can add static blocks that are created through Magento's CMS into your theme's templates and pages. Magento layout also allows you to add a static block that is created and managed by Magento's CMS tool to an area of your Magento layout.

You need to create a static block by navigating to **CMS | Static Blocks** in Magento's administration panel. This example will use a block identifier of sidebar_promise, which you will need to remember when it comes to applying the layout to display this block:

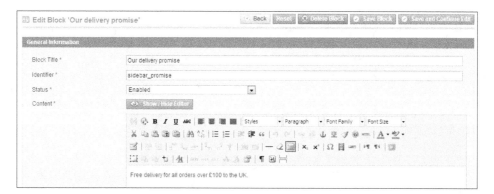

Once you have created your static block, open your theme's `local.xml` file to assign the static block you created earlier to the left sidebar using the following highlighted XML:

```xml
<?xml version="1.0"?>
<layout>
  <default>
    <reference name="left">
      <block type="cms/block" name="left.delivery">
        <action method="setBlockId">
          <block_id>sidebar_promise</block_id>
        </action>
      </block>
    </reference>
  </default>
</layout>
```

Once you have saved this change, navigate to the frontend of your store and view the page you edited to see the new block appear in the sidebar:

The static block is displayed in the lower-left corner of the sidebar

You can now style this block as you wish by introducing the necessary HTML and CSS.

# Assigning a static block to a page in Magento's CMS

You can also assign a static block to a specific page using Magento's CMS. Once you have created your static block, navigate to **CMS | Pages** and select a page you want to assign the static block to. From there, select the **Design** tab for the page and ensure that the **Layout** field is set to **2 columns with right bar**, as shown in the following screenshot:

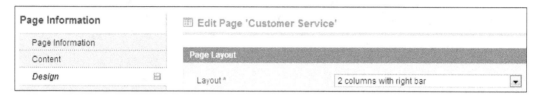

Next, add the following XML to the page's **Layout Update XML** field to assign the `sidebar_promise` static block to the right-hand side column on this page:

```
<reference name="right">
<block type="cms/block" name="right.delivery">
<action method="setBlockId"><block_id>sidebar_promise</block_id></action>
</block>
</reference>
```

Once entered, your **Design** tab for this page should look similar to the following screenshot:

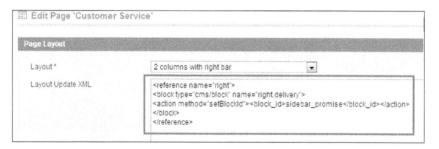

Click on the **Save Page** button at the top-right corner of the screen and view this page on the frontend of your Magento store. You will see the block is appended to the bottom of the right-hand sidebar:

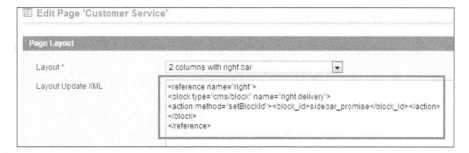

If you don't see your change appear, ensure that you refresh Magento's caches by navigating to **System | Cache Management**.

# Changing the ordering of blocks in Magento's sidebar

Apart from giving you the power to add and remove blocks from templates, the Magento layout gives you the power to reorder blocks within your pages too. There are a few ways you could rearrange the blocks in your theme's sidebar, for instance, by moving a specific block:

- Below another block
- To the very top of the list of blocks
- To the very bottom of the list of blocks

# Repositioning a block below a specific block

As an example, take the current right sidebar in your theme, which will look similar to what is shown in the following screenshot:

Firstly, you can add some simple styling to the sidebar blocks to help us distinguish them from each other. Open your theme's `styles.css` file in the `/skin/frontend/default/m18/css/` directory and add the following CSS:

```
.block {
background: #fff;
border-radius: 10px;
box-shadow: #CCC 0 10px 20px;
margin-bottom: 20px;
}
.block-title {
background: #e57d04;
color: #fff;
font-weight: bold;
}
.block-content,
.block-title {
padding: 10px;
}
```

```
.block-banner .block-content {
padding: 0;
}
```

If you now refresh your store, the blocks in the sidebar will look more distinct from each other:

Next, you will need to open your theme's `local.xml` file in the `/app/design/frontend/default/m18/layout/` directory of your Magento installation. If you want to move the **Compare Products** block above the **My Cart** callout block, you will use the `after` attribute in Magento layout to specify the block it appears after.

In Magento, the typical way to do this is to first unset the **Compare Products** block and then reinsert the block below the **My Cart** block:

```
<reference name="right">
<action method="unsetChild">
<name>catalog.compare.sidebar</name>
</action>
<block type="catalog/product_compare_sidebar" after="cart_sidebar"
name="catalog.compare.sidebar.replacement" template="catalog/product/
compare/sidebar.phtml"/>
</reference>
```

> The name values need to match the block name within Magento; one of the best ways to track down specific block names for your needs is to look through the layout files in the `/app/design/frontend/base/default/layout/` and `/app/design/frontend/default/default/layout/` directories.

The `after` value which blocks the repositioned block appears below while the `template` attribute defines which Magento template file should be used to render this block's content (in relation to the `/app/design/frontend/your-package/your-theme/template/` directory).

If you now refresh a page on your store with the right sidebar enabled, you will see the blocks' ordering has been changed:

Once again, if you can't see the change on your store, ensure that you have refreshed or disabled Magento's caches by navigating to **System | Cache Management** in your Magento store's control panel.

# Reordering a block above all other blocks

Alternatively, you can move blocks within regions of your Magento templates to the top of all other blocks. Open your theme's `local.xml` file and add the layout XML:

```
<reference name="right">
<action method="unsetChild">
<name>catalog.compare.sidebar</name>
</action>
<block type="catalog/product_compare_sidebar" before="-"
name="catalog.compare.sidebar.replacement" template="catalog/product/
compare/sidebar.phtml"/>
</reference>
```

Note the similarities with the preceding snippet; though in the previous example, you replace the `after` attribute with `before` and assign this attribute the value of `-`, which indicates it should be shown before all other blocks. If you refresh your page with the right sidebar visible, you will now see the blocks have reordered once again to show **Compare Products** at the top of the sidebar:

# Reordering a block below all other blocks

It is also possible to use this method to render blocks in your Magento template regions to position a specific block below all other blocks. Once again, open your `local.xml` file and use the following Magento layout XML to reorder the **Compare Products** block to the bottom of the blocks in the sidebar:

```
<reference name="right">
<remove name="catalog.compare.sidebar" />
<block type="catalog/product_compare_sidebar" after="-" name="catalog.
compare.sidebar.replacement" template="catalog/product/compare/
sidebar.phtml"/>
</reference>
```

Note that the preceding XML uses the `after` attribute with a value of - (hyphen) to tell Magento to place this block after all others in this region. Refresh your screen once again to see the change take effect:

# Removing unnecessary blocks from Magento's sidebar

As you can see from the previous screenshots of this chapter, there are quite a few blocks displayed in Magento's sidebars by default that you will not want to use. You can set these not to display in your theme customizing your theme's layout instructions.

Open your theme's `local.xml` file and apply the following XML:

```
<reference name="left">
<remove name="left.permanent.callout"/>
<remove name="right.newsletter"/>
<remove name="cart_sidebar"/>
<remove name="sale.reorder.sidebar"/>
</reference>

<reference name="right">
<remove name="right.permanent.callout"/>
<remove name="livechat.chat"/>
<remove name="right.poll"/>
<remove name="paypal.partner.right.logo"/>
<remove name="cart_sidebar"/>
<remove name="sale.reorder.sidebar"/>
<remove name="catalog.compare.sidebar"/>
</reference>
```

This removes commonly unused blocks in your Magento theme:

- The cart box in the sidebar
- The customer wishlist widget and "compare products" widget
- The placeholder advertisements ("callouts") in the left and right sidebars
- The list of previously viewed and compared products displayed in the right sidebar
- The newsletter subscription and customer poll widgets, and the PayPal logo included in Magento's sample widgets

If you save your `local.xml` file and look again at your Magento store, you will see these blocks have now been removed from your store:

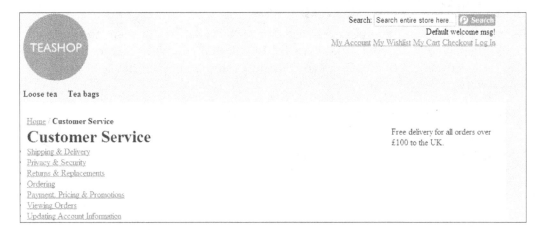

If you can't see your changes, ensure that you have refreshed or disabled Magento's caches by navigating to **System | Cache Management**.

# Customizing the home page's layout

You have seen how to apply a page layout to specific pages, but to apply a specific template to your store's home page, you can add more specific layout instructions in your theme's `local.xml` file.

The layout handle for the home page is `cms_index_index`. So, to assign the home page the one column layout, you will add the following to your Magento theme's `local.xml` file:

```
<cms_index_index>
<reference name="root">
<action method="setTemplate">
<template>page/1column.phtml</template>
</action>
</reference>
</cms_index_index>
```

Note, though, that the layout can be overwritten through Magento's CMS tool, so this is unlikely to work in practice. You can navigate to **CMS | Pages** in your Magento installation's administration panel and set your page's layout using the **Layout** drop-down field in the **Design** tab:

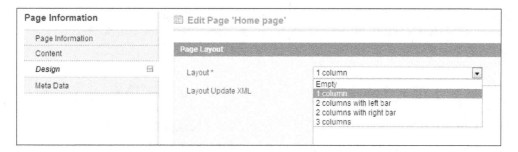

 An incomplete list of layout handles available in Magento is available at `http://www.magentocommerce.com/boards/viewthread/2471/`.

# Adding new product block to the home page

A common requirement of e-commerce stores is to display a number of newly added products on the home page; this can be useful for search engines (to encourage new products to be indexed more quickly) and customers who are visiting again to find newly added stock on your website.

## Marking products as new in Magento

Before you start making changes to your theme, ensure that you have a few products marked as "new" within Magento. To do this, log in to your Magento administration panel and navigate to **Catalog | Manage Products**. From there, select a product that you wish to mark as new. On the **General** tab, enter date values for the **Set Product as New from Date** and **Set Product as New to Date** fields that include the current date so the products are currently marked as "new" within Magento:

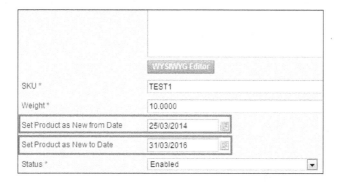

Once you have done this, click on the **Save** button at the top-right corner of your screen. You may wish to add more than one product to the new products list using this method.

# Using XML layout to add the New Products block to your store's home page

Once you have assigned some products in your store to the new products list, open your theme's local.xml file and add the following highlighted XML within the cms_index_index handle:

```
<cms_index_index>
<reference name="content">
<block type="catalog/product_new" template="catalog/product/new.
phtml">
<action method="setProductsCount"><count>3</count></action>
<action method="addColumnCountLayoutDepend"><layout>empty</
layout><count>5</count></action>
<action method="addColumnCountLayoutDepend"><layout>one_column</
layout><count>5</count></action>
<action method="addColumnCountLayoutDepend"><layout>two_columns_left</
layout><count>4</count></action>
<action method="addColumnCountLayoutDepend"><layout>two_columns_
right</layout><count>4</count></action>
<action method="addColumnCountLayoutDepend"><layout>three_columns</
layout><count>3</count></action>
</block>
</reference>
</cms_index_index>
```

If you refresh the home page, you will see the products you marked as "new" in Magento's administration panel are now visible, but they are not styled:

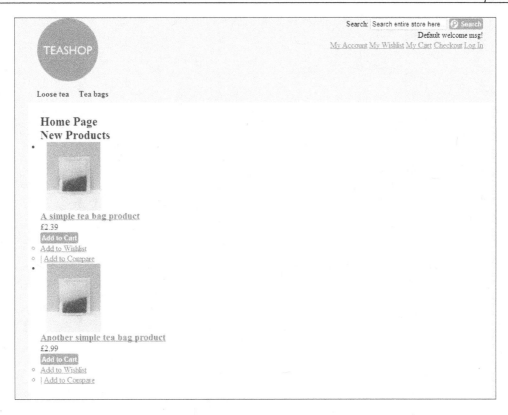

Finally, you can apply some styling to the product grid by adding the following CSS to your `styles.css` file in the `/skin/frontend/default/m18/css/` directory:

```
.products-grid {
border-bottom: 1px solid #CCC;
list-style: none;
position: relative;
}
.products-grid.last {
border-bottom: 0;
}
.products-grid li.item {
border-right: 1px #CCC solid;
float: left;
width: 138px;
padding: 12px 10px 80px;
}
```

```
.products-grid li.item.last {
border-right: none;
}
.products-grid .product-image {
display: block;
height: 135px;
margin: 0 0 10px;
width: 135px;
}
.products-grid .product-name {
color: #e57d04;
font-size: 0.9em;
font-weight: bold;
margin: 0 0 5px;
}
.products-grid .product-name a {
color:#203548;
}
.products-grid .price-box {
margin:5px 0;
}
.products-grid .availability {
line-height:21px;
}
.products-grid .actions {
position:absolute;
bottom:12px;
}

.add-to-links {
list-style: none;
font-size: 0.8em;
margin-top: 10px;
}
```

This provides a neater product grid to display your products throughout your Magento store, including the **New Products** block that now appears on the home page:

# Summary

In this chapter, you learned how using and applying Magento layout allows you to alter how Magento behaves and appears to your customers. In particular, you created a `local.xml` file to hold your theme's custom layout instructions, changed the default page template, and used Magento's CMS to change a page's layout. You also assigned a static block to a page using Magento layout and altered blocks from Magento's sidebar templates. Finally, you added a new products block to your store's home page template.

Further chapters will provide more ideas for the customization of your Magento theme, from customizing store e-mails to improving your store for mobile users.

# 5
# Social Media and Magento

So, you've begun to develop your own custom Magento 1.8 theme now. Social networks such as Twitter and Facebook are ever popular and can be a great source of new customers if used correctly on your store. This chapter covers the following topics:

- Integrating a Twitter feed into your Magento store
- Integrating a Facebook Like Box into your Magento store
- Including social share buttons in your product pages
- Integrating product videos from YouTube into the product page

## Integrating a Twitter feed into your Magento store

If you're active on Twitter, it can be worthwhile to let your customers know. While you can't (yet, anyway!) accept payment for your goods through Twitter, it can be a great way to develop a long term relationship with your store's customers and increase repeat orders.

One way you can tell customers you're active on Twitter is to place a Twitter feed that contains some of your recent tweets on your store's home page. While you need to be careful not to get in the way of your store's true content, such as your most recent products and offers, you could add the Twitter feed in the footer of your website.

# Creating your Twitter widget

To embed your tweets, you will need to create a Twitter widget. Log in to your Twitter account, navigate to `https://twitter.com/settings/widgets`, and follow the instructions given there to create a widget that contains your most recent tweets. This will create a block of code for you that looks similar to the following code:

```
<a class="twitter-timeline" href="https://twitter.com/RichardCarter"
data-widget-id="123456789999999999">Tweets by @RichardCarter</a>
<script>!function(d,s,id){var js,fjs=d.getElementsByTagName(s)
[0],p=/^http:/.test(d.location)?'http':'https';if(!d.
getElementById(id)){js=d.createElement(s);js.id=id;js.
src=p+"://platform.twitter.com/widgets.js";fjs.parentNode.
insertBefore(js,fjs);}}(document,"script","twitter-wjs");</script>
```

# Embedding your Twitter feed into a Magento template

Once you have the Twitter widget code to embed, you're ready to embed it into one of Magento's template files. This Twitter feed will be embedded in your store's footer area. So, so open your theme's `/app/design/frontend/default/m18/template/page/html/footer.phtml` file and add the highlighted section of the following code:

```
<div class="footer-about footer-col">
<?php echo $this->getLayout()->createBlock('cms/block')-
>setBlockId('footer_about')->toHtml(); ?>
<?php
$_helper = Mage::helper('catalog/category');
$_categories = $_helper->getStoreCategories();
if (count($_categories) > 0): ?>
<ul>
<?phpforeach($_categories as $_category): ?>
<li>
<a href="<?php echo $_helper->getCategoryUrl($_category) ?>">
<?php echo $_category->getName() ?>
</a>
</li>
<?phpendforeach; ?>
</ul>
<?phpendif; ?>
<a class="twitter-timeline" href="https://twitter.com/RichardCarter"
data-widget-id="123456789999999999">Tweets by @RichardCarter</a>
```

```
<script>!function(d,s,id){var js,fjs=d.getElementsByTagName(s)
[0],p=/^http:/.test(d.location)?'http':'https';if(!d.
getElementById(id)){js=d.createElement(s);js.id=id;js.
src=p+"://platform.twitter.com/widgets.js";fjs.parentNode.
insertBefore(js,fjs);}}(document,"script","twitter-wjs");</script>
</div>
```

The result of the preceding code is a Twitter feed similar to the following one embedded on your store:

 As you can see, the Twitter widget is quite cumbersome. So, it's wise to be sparing when adding this to your website. Sometimes, a simple Twitter icon that links to your account is all you need!

You could also use a static block in Magento to contain your Twitter feed; refer to *Chapter 4*, *Magento Layout*, to see how you can add a static block to a Magento template.

# Integrating a Facebook Like Box into your Magento store

Facebook is one of the world's most popular social networks; with careful integration, you can help drive your customers to your Facebook page and increase long term interaction. This will drive repeat sales and new potential customers to your store. One way to integrate your store's Facebook page into your Magento site is to embed your Facebook page's news feed into it.

# Getting the embedding code from Facebook

Getting the necessary code for embedding from Facebook is relatively easy; navigate to the Facebook Developers website at `https://developers.facebook.com/docs/plugins/like-box-for-pages`. Here, you are presented with a form. Complete the form to generate your embedding code; enter your Facebook page's URL in the **Facebook Page URL** field (the following example uses Magento's Facebook page):

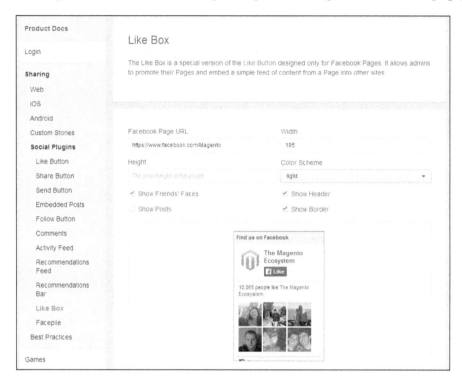

Click on the **Get Code** button on the screen to tell Facebook to generate the code you will need, and you will see a pop up with the code appear as shown in the following screenshot:

# Adding the embed code into your Magento templates

Now that you have the embedding code from Facebook, you can alter your templates to include the code snippets. The first block of code for the **JavaScript SDK** is required in the `header.phtml` file in your theme's directory at `/app/design/frontend/default/m18/template/page/html/`. Then, add it at the top of the file:

```
<div id="fb-root"></div>
<script>(function(d, s, id) {
varjs, fjs = d.getElementsByTagName(s)[0];
  if (d.getElementById(id)) return;
  js = d.createElement(s); js.id = id;
  js.src = "//connect.facebook.net/en_GB/all.js#xfbml=1";
  fjs.parentNode.insertBefore(js, fjs);
}(document, 'script', 'facebook-jssdk'));</script>
```

Next, you can add the second code snippet provided by the Facebook Developers site where you want the Facebook Like Box to appear in your page. For flexibility, you can create a static block in Magento's CMS tool to contain this code and then use the Magento XML layout to assign the static block to a template's sidebar.

Navigate to **CMS | Static Blocks** in Magento's administration panel and add a new static block by clicking on the **Add New Block** button at the top-right corner of the screen. Enter a suitable name for the new static block in the **Block Title** field and give it a value `facebook` in the **Identifier** field. Disable Magento's rich text editor tool by clicking on the **Show / Hide Editor** button above the **Content** field.

Enter in the **Content** field the second snippet of code the Facebook Developers website provided, which will be similar to the following code:

```
<div class="fb-like-box" data-href="https://www.facebook.com/Magento"
data-width="195" data-colorscheme="light" data-show-faces="true" data-
header="true" data-stream="false" data-show-border="true"></div>
```

Once complete, your new block should look like the following screenshot:

Click on the **Save Block** button to create a new block for your Facebook widget. Now that you have created the block, you can alter your Magento theme's layout files to include the block in the right-hand column of your store.

Next, open your theme's `local.xml` file located at `/app/design/frontend/ default/m18/layout/` and add the following highlighted block of XML to it. This will add the static block that contains the Facebook widget:

```
<reference name="right">
<block type="cms/block" name="cms_facebook">
<action method="setBlockId"><block_id>facebook</block_id></action>
</block>
<!--other layout instructions -->
</reference>
```

If you save this change and refresh your Magento store on a page that uses the right-hand column page layout, you will see your new Facebook widget appear in the right-hand column. This is shown in the following screenshot:

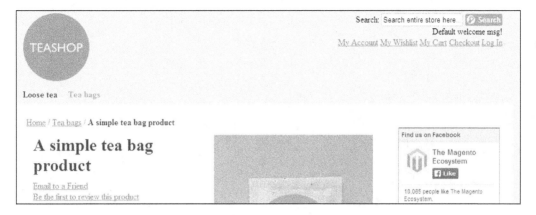

# Including social share buttons in your product pages

Particularly if you are selling to consumers rather than other businesses, you can make use of social share buttons in your product pages to help customers share the products they love with their friends on social networks such as Facebook and Twitter. One of the most convenient ways to do this is to use a third-party service such as AddThis, which also allows you to track your most shared content. This is useful to learn which products are your most-shared products within your store!

## Styling the product page a little further

Before you begin to integrate the share buttons, you can style your product page to provide a little more layout and distinction between the blocks of content. Open your theme's `styles.css` file and append the following CSS (located at `/skin/frontend/default/m18/css/`) to provide a column for the product image and a column for the introductory content of the product:

```
.product-img-box, .product-shop {
float: left;
margin: 1%;
padding: 1%;
width: 46%;
}
```

You can also add some additional CSS to style some of the elements that appear on the product view page in your Magento store:

```
.product-name {
margin-bottom: 10px;
}
.or {
color: #888;
display: block;
margin-top: 10px;
}
.add-to-box {
background: #f2f2f2;
border-radius: 10px;
margin-bottom: 10px;
padding: 10px;
}
.more-views ul {
list-style-type: none;
}
```

If you refresh a product page on your store, you will see the new layout take effect:

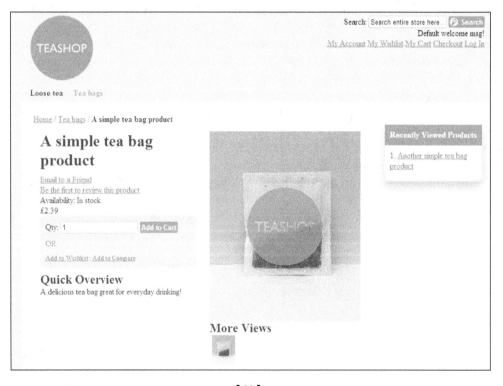

# Integrating AddThis

Now that you have styled the product page a little, you can integrate AddThis with your Magento store. You will need to get a code snippet from the AddThis website at http://www.addthis.com/get/sharing. Your snippet will look something similar to the following code:

```
<div class="addthis_toolboxaddthis_default_style ">
<a class="addthis_button_facebook_like" fb:like:layout="button_
count"></a>
<a class="addthis_button_tweet"></a>
<a class="addthis_button_pinterest_pinit"
pi:pinit:layout="horizontal"></a>
<a class="addthis_counteraddthis_pill_style"></a>
</div>
<script type="text/javascript">varaddthis_config = {"data_track_
addressbar":true};</script>
<script type="text/javascript" src="//s7.addthis.com/js/300/addthis_
widget.js#pubid=youraddthisusername"></script>
```

Once the preceding code is included in a page, this produces a social share tool that will look similar to the following screenshot:

Copy the product view template from the view.phtml file from /app/design/frontend/base/default/catalog/product/ to /app/design/frontend/default/m18/catalog/product/ and open your theme's view.phtml file for editing. You probably don't want the share buttons to obstruct the page name, add-to-cart area, or the brief description field. So, positioning the social share tool underneath those items is usually a good idea. Locate the snippet in your view.phtml file that has the following code:

```
<?php if ($_product->getShortDescription()):?>
<div class="short-description">
<h2><?php echo $this->__('Quick Overview') ?></h2>
<div class="std"><?php echo $_helper->productAttribute($_product,
nl2br($_product->getShortDescription()), 'short_description') ?></div>
</div>
<?phpendif;?>
```

Below this block, you can insert your AddThis social share tool highlighted in the following code so that the code is similar to the following block of code (the `youraddthisusername` value on the last line becomes your AddThis account's username):

```
<?php if ($_product->getShortDescription()):?>
<div class="short-description">
<h2><?php echo $this->__('Quick Overview') ?></h2>
<div class="std"><?php echo $_helper->productAttribute($_product,
nl2br($_product->getShortDescription()), 'short_description') ?></div>
</div>
<?phpendif;?>

<div class="addthis_toolboxaddthis_default_style ">
<a class="addthis_button_facebook_like" fb:like:layout="button_
count"></a>
<a class="addthis_button_tweet"></a>
<a class="addthis_button_pinterest_pinit"
pi:pinit:layout="horizontal"></a>
<a class="addthis_counteraddthis_pill_style"></a>
</div>
<script type="text/javascript">varaddthis_config = {"data_track_
addressbar":true};</script>
<script type="text/javascript" src="//s7.addthis.com/js/300/addthis_
widget.js#pubid=youraddthisusername"></script>
```

If you want to reuse this block in multiple places throughout your store, consider adding this to a static block in Magento and using Magento's XML layout to add the block as required. This is described in *Chapter 4, Magento Layout*.

Once again, refresh the product page on your Magento store and you will see the AddThis toolbar appear as shown in the following screenshot. It allows your customers to begin sharing their favorite products on their preferred social networking sites.

 If you can't see your changes, don't forget to clear your caches by navigating to **System | Cache Management**.

If you want to provide some space between other elements and the AddThis toolbar, add the following CSS to your theme's `styles.css` file:

```
.addthis_toolbox {
margin: 10px 0;
}
```

The resulting product page will now look similar to the following screenshot. You have successfully integrated social sharing tools on your Magento store's product page:

# Integrating product videos from YouTube into the product page

An increasingly common occurrence on ecommerce stores is the use of video in addition to product photography. The use of videos in product pages can help customers overcome any fears they're not buying the right item and give them a better chance to see the quality of the product they're buying. You can, of course, simply add the HTML provided by YouTube's embedding tool to your product description. However, if you want to insert your video on a specific page within your product template, you can follow the steps described in this section.

# Product attributes in Magento

Magento products are constructed from a number of attributes (different fields), such as product name, description, and price. Magento allows you to customize the attributes assigned to products, so you can add new fields to contain more information on your product. Using this method, you can add a new **Video** attribute that will contain the video embedding HTML from YouTube and then insert it into your store's product page template.

An attribute value is text or other content that relates to the attribute, for example, the attribute value for the Product Name attribute might be `Blue Tshirt`.

Magento allows you to create different types of attribute:

- **Text Field**: This is used for short lines of text.
- **Text Area**: This is used for longer blocks of text.
- **Date**: This is used to allow a date to be specified.
- **Yes/No**: This is used to allow a Boolean true or false value to be assigned to the attribute.
- **Dropdown**: This is used to allow just one selection from a list of options to be selected.
- **Multiple Select**: This is used for a combination box type to allow one or more selections to be made from a list of options provided.
- **Price**: This is used to allow a value other than the product's price, special price, tier price, and cost. These fields inherit your store's currency settings.
- **Fixed Product Tax**: This is required in some jurisdictions for certain types of products (for example, those that require an environmental tax to be added).

# Creating a new attribute for your video field

Navigate to **Catalog** | **Attributes** | **Manage Attributes** in your Magento store's control panel. From there, click on the **Add New Attribute** button located near the top-right corner of your screen:

In the **Attribute Properties** panel, enter a value in the **Attribute Code** field that will be used internally in Magento to refer this. Remember the value you enter here, as you will require it in the next step! We will use `video` as the **Attribute Code** value in this example (this is shown in the following screenshot). You can leave the remaining settings in this panel as they are to allow this newly created attribute to be used with all types of products within your store.

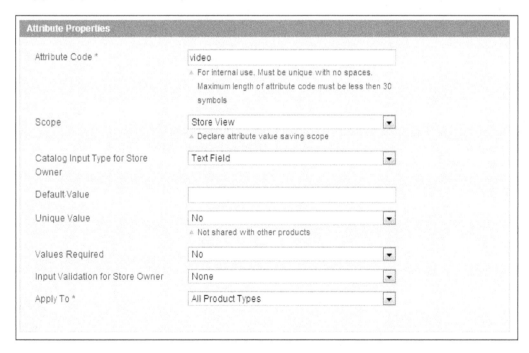

In the **Frontend Properties** panel, ensure that **Allow HTML Tags on Frontend** is set to **Yes** (you'll need this enabled to allow you to paste the YouTube embedding HTML into your store and for it to work in the template). This is shown in the following screenshot:

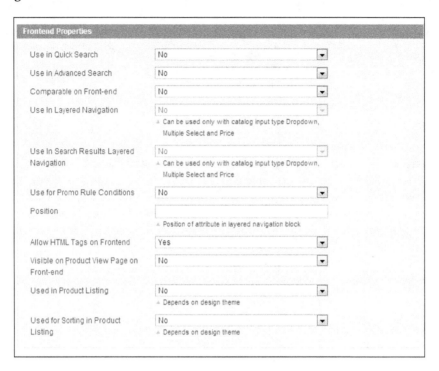

Now select the **Manage Labels / Options** tab in the left-hand column of your screen and enter a value in the **Admin** and **Default Store View** fields in the **Manage Titles** panel:

Then, click on the **Save Attribute** button located near the top-right corner of the screen. Finally, navigate to **Catalog | Attributes | Manage Attribute Sets** and select the attribute set you wish to add your new video attribute to (we will use the **Default** attribute set for this example). In the right-hand column of this screen, you will see the list of **Unassigned Attributes** with the newly created **video** attribute in this list:

Drag-and-drop this attribute into the **Groups** column under the **General** group as shown in the following screenshot:

Click on the **Save Attribute Set** button at the top-right corner of the screen to add the new **video** attribute to the attribute set.

# Adding a YouTube video to a product using the new attribute

Once you have added the new attribute to your Magento store, you can add a video to a product. Navigate to **Catalog | Manage Products** and select a product to edit (ensure that it uses one of the attribute sets you added the new video attribute to). The new **Video** field will be visible under the **General** tab:

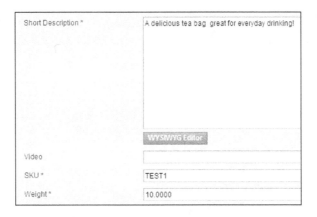

Insert the embedding code from the YouTube video you wish to use on your product page into this field. The embed code will look like the following:

```
<iframe width="320" height="240" src="//www.youtube.com/embed/
dQw4w9WgXcQ?rel=0" frameborder="0" allowfullscreen></iframe>
```

Once you have done that, click on the **Save** button to save the changes to the product.

# Inserting the video attribute into your product view template

Your final task is to allow the content of the video attribute to be displayed in your product page templates in Magento. Open your theme's `view.phtml` file from `/app/design/frontend/default/m18/catalog/product/` and locate the following snippet of code:

```
<div class="product-img-box">
<?php echo $this->getChildHtml('media') ?>
</div>
```

Add the following highlighted code to the preceding code to check whether a video for the product exists and show it if it does exist:

```
<div class="product-img-box">
<?php
$_video-html = $_product->getResource()->getAttribute('video')-
>getFrontend()->getValue($_product);
if ($_video-html) echo $_video-html ;
?>
<?php echo $this->getChildHtml('media') ?>
</div>
```

If you now refresh the product page that you have added a video to, you will see that the video appears in the same column as the product image. This is shown in the following screenshot:

# Summary

In this chapter, we looked at expanding the customization of your Magento theme to include elements from social networking sites. You learned about integrating a Twitter feed and Facebook feed into your Magento store, including social share buttons in your product pages, and integrating product videos from YouTube. In the following chapters, we will look at improving your theme for mobile devices and customizing Magento's transactional e-mail templates.

# 6
# Advanced Magento Theming

Now you have seen the basics of creating a custom Magento theme, and you will build on this using the following techniques in this chapter:

- Adding a custom print style sheet to your Magento store
- Using locales to translate labels/phrases in your store
- Using `@font-face` in Magento
- Styling Magento's layered navigation
- Creating a custom 404 "not found" error page
- Using microformats for rich snippets to enhance search engine listings

## Adding a custom print style sheet to your Magento store

So far, you've styled your Magento store for electronic screens, but what about for those customers who want to print product pages? Even in this digital age, some customers like to print details of a product and review them offline.

You can specify a separate CSS file in your Magento theme to be applied when your documents are printed. By default, Magento inherits the `print.css` file in the `/skin/frontend/default/default/css/` directory, which provides some basic styling for printed documents, such as removing navigation and the store's footer, as shown in the following screenshot:

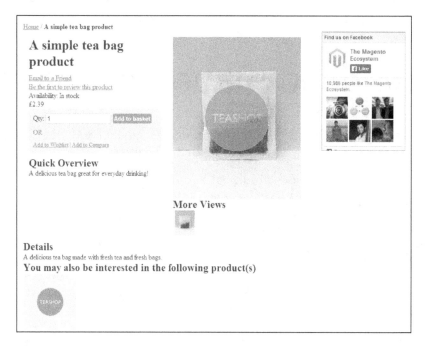

As you can see, there is still some work to be done here, as the sidebar content (the Facebook box) isn't functional or useful when the page is printed!

 You can view the print version of your Magento theme in most browsers by using the **Print preview** tool.

You can overwrite the `print.css` style sheet for your theme by creating a file called `print.css` in your theme's `css` directory (for example, `/skin/frontend/default/m18/css/`), but this will overwrite some of the work that the base print style sheet already does to help style your store's pages better for printing. Instead of overwriting this file, you can add another CSS file to add custom style instructions for printing.

To do this, open your theme's `local.xml` file (in the `/app/design/frontend/ default/m18/layout/` directory) and add the highlighted XML instruction within the `<default>` handle:

```
<default>
<reference name="head">
  <action method="addCss">
      <name>css/print-custom.css</name>
    <params>media="print"</params>
  </action>
</reference>
</default>
```

You can now create a new CSS file called `print-custom.css` in the `/skin/ frontend/default/m18/css/` directory and begin to add the print CSS specific to your new Magento theme:

```
.sidebar {
display: none;
}
```

If you now refresh the print preview of the page, you will see that the sidebar has been hidden in the following screenshot, and the content printed is much more useful!

# Using locales to translate phrases in your store

Magento supports multilingual stores, and offers locale files to allow content in the interface to be translated. Page and product content is translated through Magento's administration panel (for example, you will have an English "terms and conditions" page and a separate "terms and conditions" page for the French version of your store). Interface labels—such as the text in buttons and the user bar—can be translated by adding a locale file to your Magento theme.

At the moment, our Magento theme displays the text as **Add to Cart** on the product screen:

By using Magento locale files, you can change the wording to something more appropriate for your store; in the following example, **Add to Cart** will be changed to **Add to basket**.

# Creating a Magento locale file

A Magento locale file is a **Comma Separate Values (CSV)** file, which contains alternate translations for specified labels in your store's interface. The default text for this phrase is in the left-hand column; the right-hand column contains the new translation for this text.

 You can download the official locale files for Magento in many languages from `http://www.magentocommerce.com/translations`.

Create a file called `translate.csv` in the `/app/design/frontend/default/m18/locale/en_GB/` directory. The last directory's name equates to the locale language's ISO 639 code; en_GB indicates that this is a British English translation. Add the following line for a change in the button's label on the product page highlighted above:

```
"Add to Cart", "Add to basket"
```

You can add more translations for your store's theme in this locale file by adding one phrase per line:

```
"Add to Cart", "Add to basket"
"My Cart", "My basket"
"Cart", "Basket"
```

You now need to navigate to **System | Configuration**, and select **Locale Options** under the **General** tab to see the value of the **Locale** field; in the following screenshot, it is set to **English (United Kingdom)**:

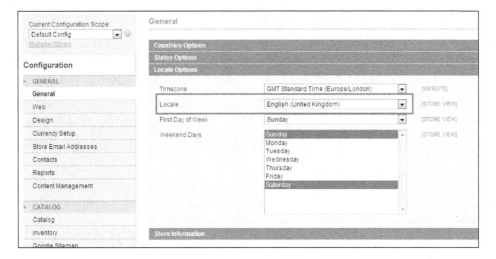

If you have changed the value of **Locale**, click on the **Save Config** button at the top-right corner of the screen and refresh your store once you've saved these changes. You should now be able to see the new translations, as shown in the following screenshot:

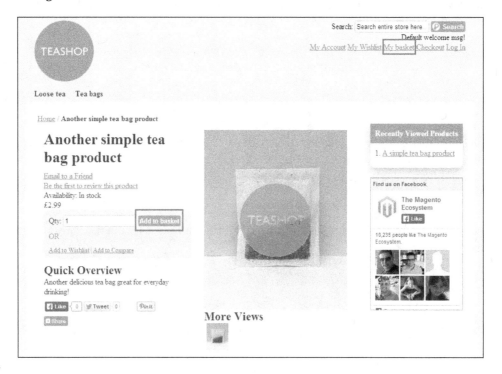

## The translate function

Only the text filtered through the __() function, which is an alias (alternate name) of the translate() function, is translated in this way. For example, the following code snippet will allow you to translate the text of the heading through locale files:

```
<h2><?php echo $this->__('Create an Account') ?></h2>
```

Alternatively, the following example, which does not use the __() function, will not use the alternate text provided in the locale file:

```
<h2>Create an Account</h2>
```

You can also enable inline translation for your Magento store by navigating to **System | Configuration | Developer | Translate Inline**.

# Using Google Web Fonts and @font-face

With the advent of the `@font-face` support across browsers, you can use custom fonts from services such as Google Web Fonts (`https://www.google.com/fonts/`) in your Magento theme.

## Including Google Web Font in your store's theme

Once you have selected a font to use, copy the code that Google Fonts provides to embed the CSS, which will look something like the following:

```
<link href='//fonts.googleapis.com/css?family=PT+Sans'
rel='stylesheet' type='text/css'>
```

Navigate to **System** | **Configuration** in your Magento store's administration panel and paste this in the **Miscellaneous Scripts** field, which is in the **HTML Head** panel under the **Design** tab, as shown in the following screenshot:

Click on the **Save Config** button at the top-right corner of the screen to save this change.

This step ensures that the font is available to be used in your theme; the next step is to use the font in your theme's style sheets.

Google's Web Font performance is okay for desktop visitors, but may slow down your store for mobile/tablet visitors on limited connections. As such, it will be better to host the EOT, WOFF of TTF font files used in your theme's `@font-face` rules locally on your store's server (or via a Content Distribution Network).

# Referencing Google Web Font in your Magento theme's style sheet

Open your theme's `styles.css` file (in the `/skin/frontend/default/m18/css/` directory) and you can use the font-family attribute to change the font. In this example, the font is changed through the website using the `body` element:

```
body {
font-family: "PT Sans", "Alike", "Times New Roman", serif;
}
```

Once you have saved this, you will see the new font from the Google Fonts service being used throughout your Magento theme:

# Styling Magento's layered navigation

One of Magento's most used features is layered navigation, which allows customers to filter products at a category level based on your products' attributes (such as color, price, and size).

# Enabling layered navigation in Magento categories

Before you can style Magento's layered navigation, you will need to ensure that your categories are configured to allow layered navigation.

To do this, log in to your Magento administration panel and navigate to **Catalog | Manage Categories**. From there, select the category you wish to enable layered navigation for, open the **Display Settings** tab, and set the **Is Anchor** field to **Yes**, as shown in the following screenshot:

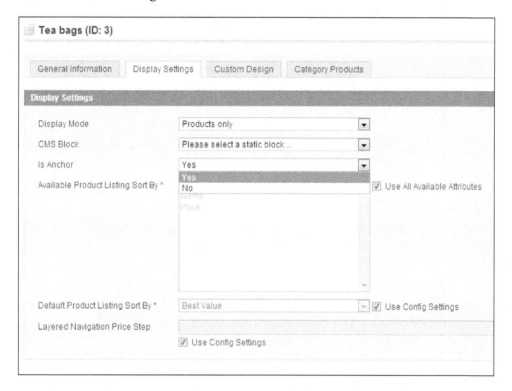

Click on the **Save Category** button at the top-right corner of the screen to assign this change to the category.

# Assigning attributes for layered navigation

Next, you need to ensure that the attributes used for the products in the category you altered previously are available for use in layered navigation. Navigate to **Catalog | Attributes | Manage Attributes** and select an attribute from the list (the example shown below uses **price** since this is used by products within our existing **Tea bags** category).

In the **Frontend Properties** panel, set the **Use In Layered Navigation** field to **Filterable (with results)** as shown in the following screenshot:

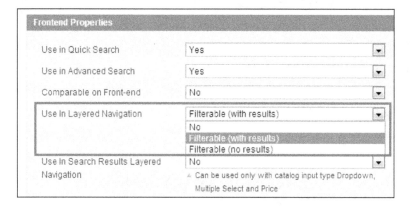

 Setting this to **Filterable (no results)** will show attribute values in the layered navigation even if there are no results.

# Creating a custom 404 "not found" error page

Even the best designed stores can lead customers to pages that don't exist any more, and customizing your **Not Found** page template can be a good way to retain customers who have lost their way.

# Altering the error page's content

The content of the Magento's error page is stored in the Magento's CMS tool, so you can start altering content here by navigating to **CMS | Manage Pages** and locating the **404 Not Found 1** page, as shown in the following screenshot:

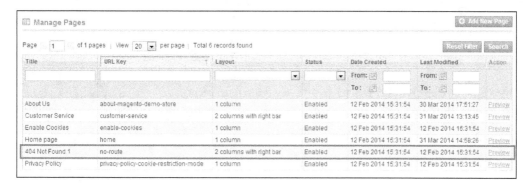

In the **Content** tab, customize your content for the error page. The following example used the **Recently Viewed Products** widget to display a selection of products the customer may be interested in:

Click on the **Save Page** button at the top-right corner of the screen and you'll see your new content appear when you try to visit a page that doesn't exist on your store:

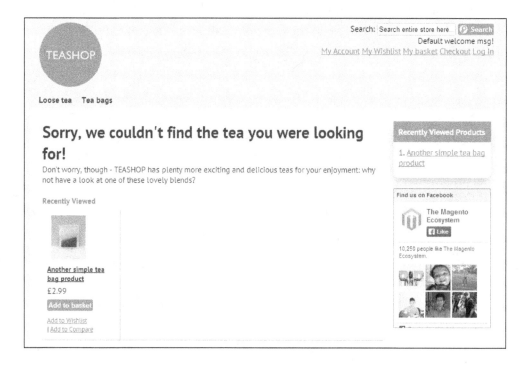

To minimize the clutter on this page and help the customer find what they're looking for, you can set the error page's **Page Layout** under the **Design** tab in Magento's CMS tool to **1 column**, as shown in the following screenshot:

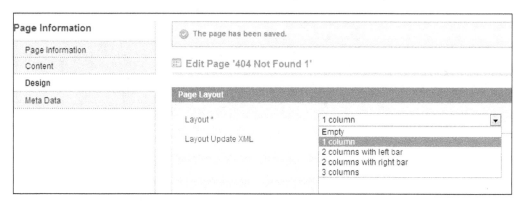

Once again, click on the **Save Page** button at the top-right corner of your screen to set the changed page layout. Finally, you can add a background image to your error page to further customize it and reassure customers a little. Open your theme's `styles.css` file from `/skin/frontend/default/m18/css/` and add the following CSS to apply the `404_bg.png` image in `/skin/frontend/default/m18/images/` to the error page template:

```
body.cms-index-noroute .main {
background: #fff url("../images/404_bg.png") no-repeat top center;
padding-top: 200px;
}
```

Once you have saved the change to the CSS and new image, refresh the error page to see the change take effect, as shown in the following screenshot:

That's it! Your Magento store's custom 404 error page is now complete.

# Using snippets to enhance search engine listings

Rich snippets are an enhanced way of providing information about the type of content on your website to search engines.

For example, rich snippets can allow search engines such as Google to display product ratings on the search engine results page, such as the Google search engine listing for a product on www.lego.com highlighted at the bottom of the following screenshot (below the paid advertisements):

Rich snippets on the website allow Google to display the star rating for the product alongside the overall rating and number of reviews.

>
> For more information on rich snippets, visit https://support.google.com/webmasters/answer/99170.

To implement the ratings-rich snippet, copy the summary.phtml file in the app/
design/frontend/base/default/template/review/helper/ folder to app/
design/frontend/default/m18/template/review/helper/, and open it to
include the following highlighted code:

```
<div itemprop="aggregateRating" itemscope itemtype="http://schema.org/
AggregateRating">
<?php if ($this->getReviewsCount()): ?>
<meta itemprop="ratingValue" content="<?php echo $this-
>getRatingSummary(); ?>"/>
<meta itemprop="reviewCount" content="<?php echo $this-
>getReviewsCount(); ?>" />
<meta itemprop="worstRating" content="0"/>
<meta itemprop="bestRating" content="100"/>
<div class="ratings">
<?php if ($this->getRatingSummary()):?>
<div class="rating-box">
<div class="rating" style="width:<?php echo $this->getRatingSummary()
?>%"></div>
</div>
<?php endif;?>
<p class="rating-links">
<a href="<?php echo $this->getReviewsUrl() ?>"><?php echo $this->__
('%d Review(s)', $this->getReviewsCount()) ?></a>
<span class="separator">|</span>
<a href="<?php echo $this->getReviewsUrl() ?>#review-form"><?php echo
$this->__('Add Your Review') ?></a>
</p>
</div>
<?php elseif ($this->getDisplayIfEmpty()): ?>
<p class="no-rating"><a href="<?php echo $this->getReviewsUrl()
?>#review-form"><?php echo $this->__('Be the first to review this
product') ?></a></p>
<?php endif; ?>
</div>
```

Save this file to your Magento store's theme and your rich snippet is ready to go.

 Remember, including the preceding code is only a request for
search engines to display this information in their results list,
and they might not necessarily use this.

# Summary

In this chapter, you looked at a range of more advanced techniques to customize your Magento theme with styling your Magento store further for print, using Magento locales to alter interface text, using `@font-face` from Google Web Fonts, styling Magento's layered navigation, creating a custom 404 "not found" error page, and using microformats for rich snippets to enhance search engine listings.

Further chapters look at improving your Magento store for mobile and tablet devices and customizing Magento's e-mail templates that are sent to customers.

# 7
# Magento Theming for Mobile and Tablet Devices

So far, your new Magento theme has focused on building a custom design for your store for devices with larger screens, such as desktop computers and laptops. In this chapter, you will start customizing your Magento theme for devices with different screen sizes, such as smartphones and tablet computers. We will cover the following topics:

- Using CSS media queries to create breakpoints for different device widths
- Making images responsive for your Magento theme
- Developing responsive navigation for your Magento theme
- Adding mobile homepage icons for Windows and Apple devices to your Magento theme

## Using CSS media queries to create breakpoints for different device widths

One of the ways in which you can get your Magento theme to adapt to your customer's device and provide them with an experience more tailored to their needs is to use CSS media queries to alter the style and layout of your Magento store for different screen sizes.

# Adding the meta viewport element to your Magento theme

Firstly, you will need to add the meta `viewport` element to the `<head>` element of your Magento theme. This will tell the device viewing your store to fit the store to the width of the available device's screen.

Open your theme's `local.xml` file under `/app/design/frontend/default/m18/ layout/` and add the XML highlighted in the following code within the `<default>` handle of the `<reference name="head">` element:

```
<default>
  <reference name="head">
    <block type="core/text" name="meta.viewport">
      <action method="setText">
      <meta><![CDATA[<meta name="viewport" content="width=device-
      width, initial-scale=1.0" />]]></meta>
      </action>
    </block>
  </reference>
</default>
```

Once you have saved this file, you can begin to work on CSS within your media query.

# Adding a CSS media query to your style sheet

Open your theme's `styles.css` file (located in the `/skin/frontend/default/m18/ css/` directory), and add the following CSS towards the bottom of your file:

```
@media only screen and (min-width: 50em) {
/* Your CSS applied only to larger screens goes here */
}
```

> Note that support for media queries in older browsers is limited; visit `http://caniuse.com/css-mediaqueries` for more details.

The CSS you add between the curly braces of the `@media` query here is applied only to devices that are using a `screen` media type and have a minimum width of `50em`—roughly equivalent to most larger desktop computer monitors.

For larger screens, the background of your theme is currently looking a little bare, as you can see in the following screenshot. There is currently a lot of space around the page itself.

You can provide a background image for the `.main-container` element of your store that appears only for larger-screened devices by including the following CSS in your theme's `styles.css` file:

```
@media only screen and (min-width: 50em) {
  .main-container {
  background: #f6f6f6 url("../images/body_bg.png") repeat center
center;
  }
}
```

If you now refresh your store, you'll see the new pattern take effect as shown in the following screenshot:

As always, if you can't see your changes, clear Magento's caches by navigating to **System | Cache Management**.

By using CSS media queries such as the preceding one, you can create a responsive Magento theme for your store—defining different layouts to better organize your store's content for those on different sized screens. To do this, first comment out the widths defined outside the media query you just created, which will collapse the layout for your theme in to a single column for devices with smaller screens:

```
.wrapper {
/* min-width:954px; */
}
```

```css
.main {
background:#fff;
color: #333;
margin:0 auto;
min-height:400px;
padding:25px 25px 80px;
text-align:left;
/* width:900px; */
}
.col-left {
float:left;
padding:0 0 1px;
/* width:195px; */
}
.col-main {
float:left;
padding:0 0 1px;
/* width:685px; */
}
.col-right {
float:right;
padding:0 0 1px;
/* width:195px; */
}
.col1-layout .col-main {
float:none;
width:auto
}
.col3-layout .col-main {
margin-left:17px;
/* width:475px; */
}
.col3-layout .col-wrapper {
float:left;
/* width:687px; */
}
```

So, on smaller screen devices (with a width less than the `50em` you defined in the media query earlier), you will see the simplified layout:

If you do not define some widths for the columns in your Magento theme within the media query you created earlier, this is how your store will appear on larger screens too. To rectify this, open your theme's `styles.css` file once again and add the following CSS within the media query:

```
.header, #nav, .footer {
margin: 0 auto;
max-width: 60em;
width: 100%;
}
.main-col, .col-right, .col-left {
margin: 0 1%;
padding: 1%;
}
```

```
.main {
width:900px;
}
.col-left, .col-right {
width: 21%;
}
.col-main {
width: 71%;
}
.col1-layout .col-main {
float:none;
width:auto;
}
.col3-layout .col-main {
width: 46%;
}
.col3-layout .col-wrapper {
float:left;
width: 71%;
}
```

This provides browsers with enough styling to display your store's content as columns for customers who use larger screens like your original Magento theme did before you added the media query to your style sheet. If you now view your Magento theme on a larger screen, you'll see that the layout is back to its previous state as shown in the following screenshot:

That's it! You have the basics of media queries working in your Magento theme now, and you can add and adapt CSS as your store's design requires!

# Making images responsive for your Magento theme

Images are very important on your Magento store to ensure that your customers can see what they're buying. If you look at a product page on your Magento store at the moment, you'll see that the product image hugely overflows the column's width available to it, as you can see from the highlighted portion of the following screenshot:

The easiest way to ensure that your store's images will be resized to sensible dimensions is to set the max-width attribute of the img element to 100% to ensure no image becomes larger than its container.

Open your theme's `styles.css` file in the `/skin/frontend/default/m18/css/` directory and add the following CSS to it to help ensure images are resized to the width they have available in the page's layout, their height-to-width ratio is retained, and images are not stretched out of proportion:

```
img,
img[height],
img[style],
img[width],
img#image {
height: auto !important;
max-width: 100% !important;
width: auto !important;
}
```

Once you have saved this addition, refresh your product page again and you'll see that your product photograph is constrained to the width it has available, as follows:

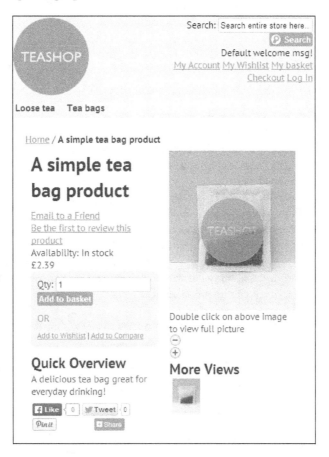

# Developing responsive navigation

Another critical area for all customers is your navigation—they need to be able to find the products they are looking for easily, after all. Mobiles, tablets, and devices with smaller screens present new challenges in terms of how to present the navigation in a clear way so that users on touchscreen devices will find it easy to interact with.

Firstly, you will need to move the current navigational styling in to the media query for larger screens. So, copy the following CSS code in to the media query you created earlier in this chapter:

```
@media only screen and (min-width: 50em) {
  #nav li.over{z-index:998}
  #nav a,#nav a:hover{display:block;line-height:1.3em;text-
decoration:none}
  #nav span{cursor:pointer;display:block;white-space:nowrap}
  #nav li ul span{white-space:normal}
  #nav ul li.parent a{background: none}
  #nav ul li.parent li a{background-image:none}
  #nav a{color:#333;float:left;font-weight:700;padding:5px 12px 6px
8px}
  #nav ul li,#nav ul li.active{background:#e57d04;float:none;margin:0;
padding-bottom:1px}
  #nav ul li.last{padding-bottom:0}
  #nav ul a,#nav ul a:hover{background:none;float:none;padding:0}
  #nav ul li a{background:#fff;font-weight:400!important}
  #nav ul,#nav div{border:1px solid #ccc;left:-10000px;position:absolu
te;top:27px;width:15em}
  #nav div ul{border:none;position:static;width:auto}
  #nav ul ul,#nav ul div{top:5px}
  #nav ul li a:hover{background:#e57d04}
  #nav ul li a,#nav ul li a:hover{color:#333!important}
  #nav ul span,#nav ul li.last li span{padding:3px 15px 4px}
  #nav li ul.shown-sub,#nav li div.shown-sub{left:0;z-index:999}
  #nav li .shown-sub ul.shown-sub,#nav li .shown-sub li div.shown-
sub{left:100px}
  #nav li.active a,#nav li.over a,#nav a:hover{color:#e57d04}
}
```

Next, you can define some styles inside a new media query to style how the navigation appears for devices with smaller screens:

```
@media only screen and (max-width: 49.99999em) {
  #nav a {
  color: #333;
```

```
display: inline-block;
padding: 0.25em 0.5em;
text-decoration: none;
}
#nav a:hover {
color: #aaa;
text-decoration: underline;
}
#nav ul {
display: inline;
}
#nav li {
display: inline;
float: left;
margin: 0 1%;
}
#nav ul.level0 {
display: inline;
}
#nav ul.level0 li {
float: none;
width: 100%;
}
#nav ul.level0 a {
color: #777;
font-size: 0.9em;
}
}
```

Including the CSS in a media query for screen widths less than 49.9999em means that this CSS won't clash with the other CSS for drop-down navigations for larger screens. This is shown in the following screenshot:

On a device with a smaller screen, the navigation is displayed as you defined it in the smaller media query, making it easier for customers to find their desired product category.

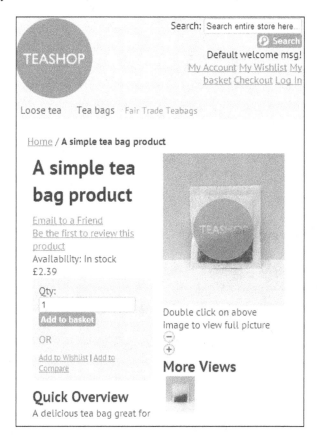

# Adding mobile icons for Windows and Apple devices

With the increasing popularity of smartphones, it's not enough to just provide a favorites icon any more; these don't work as effectively on mobile devices, but you can provide alternate icons for use on Apple, Android, and Windows devices.

# Adding an Apple home icon to your Magento store

You can specify the Apple icon that will be used when customers save your store to their device's home screen with the addition of elements to your store's `<head>` element.

 Android devices will also make use of these icons as long as the `rel` value in the link elements that reference the icons are set to `rel=apple-touch-icon` or `rel=apple-touch-icon-precomposed`.

Copy the `head.phtml` file under `/app/design/frontend/base/default/template/page/html/` to `/app/design/frontend/default/m18/template/page/html/`. Open your theme's `head.phtml` file and insert the following code at the bottom of the file to cater for the variety of sizes Apple devices can use:

```
<link rel="apple-touch-icon" href="<?php echo $this->getSkinUrl('images/icon-iphone.png') ?>" />
<link rel="apple-touch-icon" sizes="72x72" href="<?php echo $this->getSkinUrl('images/icon-ipad.png') ?>" />
<link rel="apple-touch-icon" sizes="114x114" href="<?php echo $this->getSkinUrl('images/icon-iphone_retina.png') ?>" />
<link rel="apple-touch-icon" sizes="144x144" href="<?php echo $this->getSkinUrl('images/icon-ipad-retina.png') ?>" />
```

Once you have done this, you'll need to save the icon images in your theme's `/images/` directory. You will require the following sizes:

- 57 x 57 pixels for iPhones
- 72 x 72 pixels for iPads
- 114 x 144 pixels for iPhones with retina displays
- 144 x 144 pixels for iPads with retina displays

If you now refresh your store and use the **Add To Home Screen** option in your browser, and you will see that the appropriate icon is used:

# Adding a Windows icon to your Magento store

Microsoft also allows you to specify an icon used in Internet Explorer in Windows 8 and above. Edit your theme's `head.phtml` file again, which is located in the `/app/design/frontend/default/m18/template/page/html/` directory. At the bottom of the file, add the following lines:

```
<meta name="msapplication-TileColor" content="#7F6A00"/>
<meta name="msapplication-TileImage" content="<?php echo $this->getSkinUrl('images/icon-windows.png') ?>"/>
```

Save your icon image as 64 x 64 pixels in your theme's image directory. You can specify the `TileColor` value too to define the color of the block that will contain the icon on Window's tile system.

# Summary

This chapter introduced some methods to improve your store for visitors on a range of devices. This allows you to use CSS media queries to create breakpoints for different device widths, make images responsive, develop responsive navigation for your Magento theme, and add mobile homepage icons for Windows and Apple devices to your Magento theme.

In the next chapter, you will learn how to customize Magento's transactional e-mails to help you further improve customers' experience of your store.

# Magento E-mail Templates

**8**

So far, you've looked at styling your Magento store for customers, but what about the transaction e-mails Magento sends your customers when they place an order? This chapter covers the following topics:

- Changing the e-mail template logo
- Altering colors of the e-mail templates
- Altering variables in Magento e-mail templates
- Adding static block content to your Magento e-mail templates
- Integrating a MailChimp subscription form into your Magento store
- Integrating a Campaign Monitor subscription form into your Magento store

## Working with Magento e-mail templates

Working with e-mail templates is quite different than working with websites, so you may find the following information of use in this chapter:

- Customizing e-mail markup is a tricky business: the HTML used in e-mail templates needs to follow strict guidelines. You may find Campaign Monitor's resources at `https://www.campaignmonitor.com/resources/will-it-work/`.

- Various e-mail clients will display the e-mails in various ways, much like different browsers can display the same website differently.

- It is always recommended to retain as much as possible from Magento's default e-mail templates in order to make sure the mails are displayed correctly on as many clients as possible. This will also make the Magento upgrade progress much easier for you!

- Bear in mind that most (if not all) e-mail programs don't display images by default. Be careful that your e-mails' core messages are contained within text in your e-mail and not in images!

# Changing the e-mail template logo

First thing's first: you'll want the e-mails your Magento store sends to customers to use your store's logo, so you will need to configure this in Magento's control panel.

At the moment, the order confirmation e-mail will look similar to the following template, using Magento's own logo and a placeholder store name if you haven't configured your Magento store fully yet:

 Magento®

## Hello, Richard Carter

Thank you for your order from Main Website Store. Once your package ships we will send an email with a link to track your order. You can check the status of your order by logging into your account. If you have any questions about your order please contact us at support@example.com or call us at Monday - Friday, 8am - 5pm PST.
Your order confirmation is below. Thank you again for your business.

### Your Order #100000002 (placed on 19 May 2014 11:16:08 BST)

**Billing Information:**

Richard Carter
Adamson House
Newcastle, NE1 1SG
United Kingdom
T: 01913047158

**Payment Method:**

Cash On Delivery

**Shipping Information:**

Richard Carter
Adamson House
Newcastle, NE1 1SG
United Kingdom
T: 01913047158

**Shipping Method:**

Flat Rate - Fixed

| Item | Sku | Qty | Subtotal |
|------|-----|-----|----------|
| A simple tea bag product | TEST1 | 1 | £2.39 |
| Another simple tea bag product | TEST2 | 1 | £2.99 |
| | | Subtotal | £5.38 |
| | | Shipping & Handling | £10.00 |
| | | Grand Total (Excl.Tax) | £14.98 |
| | | VAT Standard (20%) | £0.40 |
| | | Tax | £0.40 |
| | | Grand Total (Incl.Tax) | £15.38 |

Thank you, **Main Website Store**

Once you are logged into your Magento administration panel, navigate to **System |
Configuration**. From here, select the **Design** tab in the left-hand column, as shown in
the following screenshot:

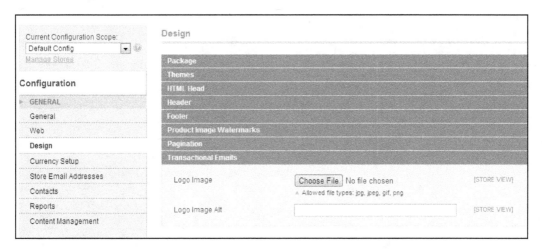

Expand the **Transactional Emails** panel, and you will see that you are provided with
two options:

1. One to change the image used for the logo in the e-mail templates.
2. One to change the `alt` text used for the logo.

Select the logo image you wish to use, and populate the **Logo Image Alt** field with a
suitable value, as shown in the following screenshot:

Once you have done this, click on the **Save Config** button. If you now cause Magento to send an order confirmation e-mail again, you will see your logo appear in the e-mail template:

 To change the e-mail addresses used in these e-mails, you need to configure them by navigating to **System | Configuration** under the **Store Email Addresses** tab.

# Sending test transactional e-mails

The easiest way to test your e-mail template is to use the **Send Email** function. Navigate to **Sales | Orders**, and select an existing order made through your Magento store, and click on the **Send Email** button at the top-right corner of the order details screen, as shown in the following screenshot:

A pop-up message will appear asking you to confirm this; click on **OK**. This will cause another order confirmation e-mail to be sent to the customer's e-mail address, allowing you to test changes to your store's e-mail templates.

# Changing the color scheme of your Magento transaction e-mail templates

Now that you've changed the logo used in Magento's transactional e-mail templates, you may also want to change your e-mail template's color scheme.

## Loading a Magento e-mail template

Navigate to **System | Transactional Emails**, and click on the **Add New Template** button at the top-right corner of the screen, as shown in the following screenshot:

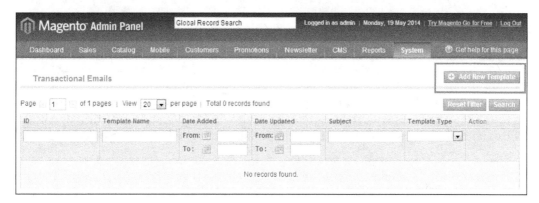

From there, select an e-mail template you wish to overwrite; the following example uses the **New Order** template, which acts as the order confirmation e-mail template:

Click on the **Load Template** button, which will populate the panel below with the current contents of this e-mail template for you to alter. Firstly, populate the **Template Name** field as we're overwriting the **New Order** template. This will be New Order v2, as shown in the following screenshot:

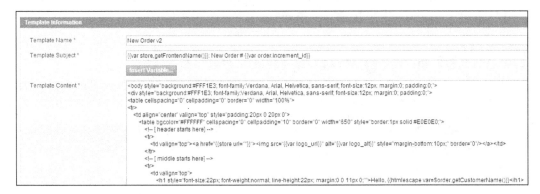

Next, in the **Template Content** field, you can overwrite any color references you need in the style attributes within the e-mail template's HTML. Examine the first two lines of this field and you will see HTML that looks similar to the following code:

```
<body style="background:#F6F6F6; font-family:Verdana, Arial,
Helvetica, sans-serif; font-size:12px; margin:0; padding:0;">
<div style="background:#F6F6F6; font-family:Verdana, Arial, Helvetica,
sans-serif; font-size:12px; margin:0; padding:0;">
```

To change the background color to a pale orange rather than the current light gray, you can make the changes in the code highlighted below:

```
<body style="background:#FFF1E3; font-family:Verdana, Arial,
Helvetica, sans-serif; font-size:12px; margin:0; padding:0;">
<div style="background:#FFF1E3; font-family:Verdana, Arial, Helvetica,
sans-serif; font-size:12px; margin:0; padding:0;">
```

If you now click on the **Save Template** button at the top-right corner of the screen, your changes will be saved. Your next task is to assign your new e-mail template to the **New Order** transaction in Magento.

# Editing Magento e-mail templates through your theme

You can also edit your theme's e-mail templates by providing e-mail template files in your theme. The base e-mail template files in Magento are located at /app/locale/ en_US/template/email. As with all core Magento files, do not edit these directly; copy them to your theme's locale directory. In the example theme provided with this book, you can copy the e-mail templates into /app/design/frontend/default/ m18/locale/en_US/template/email/.

# Assigning an e-mail template to a transaction in Magento

Navigate to **System | Configuration** and select the **Sales Emails** tab in the left-hand column. Expand the **New Order** panel and select your new e-mail template from the dropdown next to **New Order Confirmation Template**:

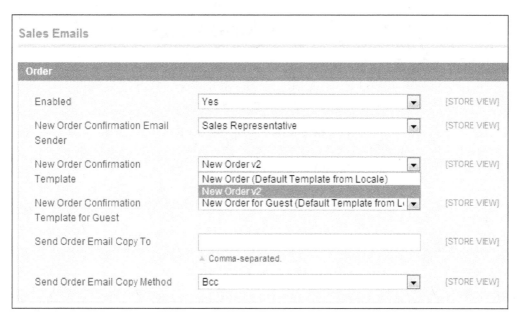

Click on the **Save Config** button at the top-right corner of the screen and resend the new order e-mail to see the changes to the template's background color appear:

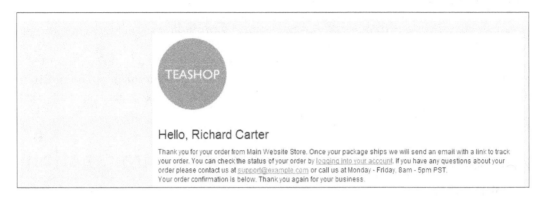

You can overwrite other e-mail templates Magento sends in a similar fashion to fully customize your store.

# Altering variables in Magento e-mail templates

You've now seen how and where to alter some of the basic HTML behind Magento's e-mail templates, but sometimes a little more customization is required.

Navigate to **System | Transactional Emails** and select the **New Order v2** template you created in the previous section of this chapter to begin editing it to use the customer's first name, rather than their full name, as it is currently displayed:

Hello, Richard Carter

Thank you for your order from Main Website Store. Once your package ships we will send an email with a link to track your order. You can check the status of your order by logging into your account. If you have any questions about your order please contact us at support@example.com or call us at Monday - Friday, 8am - 5pm PST.
Your order confirmation is below. Thank you again for your business.

In the **Template Content** field, locate the following line, which adds the customer greeting line:

```
<h1 style="font-size:22px; font-weight:normal; line-
height:22px; margin:0 0 11px 0;"">Hello, {{htmlescape var=$order.
getCustomerName()}}</h1>
```

# Magento Insert Variable pop up

Magento provides some variables in the pop up that is shown if you click on the **Insert Variable** button above the **Template Content** field as you can see in the following screenshot:

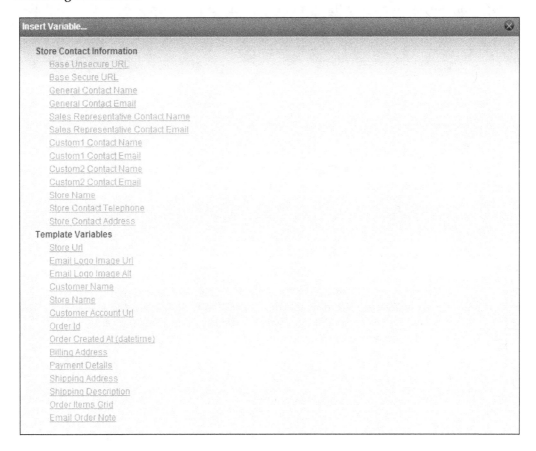

# Using the customer's first name only in e-mail templates

The customer's first name is not listed here, so you will manually need to change the code highlighted above to:

```
<h1 style="font-size:22px; font-weight:normal; line-
height:22px; margin:0 0 11px 0;"">Hello, {{htmlescape var=$order.
getCustomerFirstname()}}</h1>
```

Once you have made this change, click on the **Save Template** button at the top-right corner of the screen. If you send the e-mail confirmation order again to test your change, you will see that only the customer's first name is displayed in the template, as shown in the following screenshot:

Hello, Richard

Thank you for your order from Main Website Store. Once your package ships we will send an email with a link to track your order. You can check the status of your order by logging into your account. If you have any questions about your order please contact us at support@example.com or call us at Monday - Friday, 8am - 5pm PST. Your order confirmation is below. Thank you again for your business.

 Don't forget that you have to assign the new template by navigating to the **System | Configuration | Sales Emails** section of the Magento administration panel, if you haven't already, to see this template sent in place of the default template.

# Adding a static block to a Magento transactional e-mail template

You can take customizing your Magento transactional e-mail templates even further by adding static blocks to the templates.

## Creating the static block

Firstly, you will need to create a static block you wish to insert into your Magento e-mail template. Navigate to **CMS | Static Blocks** and click on the **Add New Block** button at the top-right corner of the screen.

Provide **Block Title** and **Identifier** (the example uses email_ as a prefix to help you know where the block is used), as shown in the following screenshot:

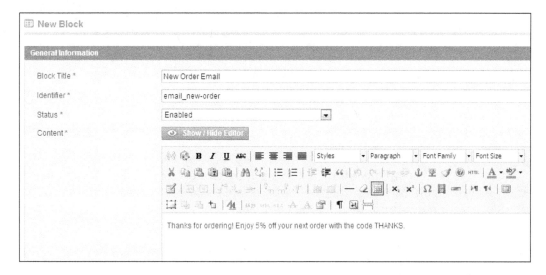

Use the **Content** field to add content you would like to appear within the e-mail template itself. Once you're finished, click on the **Save Block** button at the top-right corner of the screen.

# Adding the static block to the e-mail template

Once again, navigate to **System | Transactional Emails** and edit the **New Order v2** template you created earlier. Locate the following code in the **Template Content** field:

```
If you have any questions about your order please contact us at
<a href="mailto:{{config path='trans_email/ident_support/email'}}"
style="color:#1E7EC8;">{{config path='trans_email/ident_support/
email'}}</a> or call us at <span class="nobr">{{config path='general/
store_information/phone'}}</span> Monday - Friday, 8am - 5pm PST.
</p>
<p style="font-size:12px; line-height:16px; margin:0;">
Your order confirmation is below. Thank you again for your business.
</p>
```

Change this to include the following highlighted code, where the `block_id` value matches the **Identifier** value of the static block you created:

```
If you have any questions about your order please contact us at
<a href="mailto:{{config path='trans_email/ident_support/email'}}"
style="color:#1E7EC8;">{{config path='trans_email/ident_support/
email'}}</a> or call us at <span class="nobr">{{config path='general/
store_information/phone'}}</span> Monday - Friday, 8am - 5pm PST.
</p>
{{block type="cms/block" block_id="email_new-order" }}
<p style="font-size:12px; line-height:16px; margin:0;">
Your order confirmation is below. Thank you again for your business.
</p>
```

Click on the **Save Template** button at the top-right corner of the screen once more and generate a new e-mail for the new order template. You will see that the static block's content now appears within the template:

Hello, Richard

Thank you for your order from Main Website Store. Once your package ships we will send an email with a link to track your order. You can check the status of your order by logging into your account. If you have any questions about your order please contact us at support@example.com or call us at Monday - Friday, 8am - 5pm PST.

Thanks for ordering! Enjoy 5% off your next order with the code THANKS.

Your order confirmation is below. Thank you again for your business.

# Integrating the MailChimp subscription form into your Magento store

E-mails related to your e-commerce website don't stop at order e-mails to customers, although e-mail marketing can play an important role in encouraging repeat orders and generating new business for your store.

One popular e-mail marketing system is MailChimp, and you can create a static block on your store and use this throughout your store to entice customers to subscribe for offers and articles on your chosen sector.

 Alternatively, you can synchronize your newsletter subscribers through Magento using the MailChimp plugin for Magento at `http://connect.mailchimp.com/integrations/magento`.

Firstly, you will need to get the HTML for MailChimp's subscription form: log in to your account on `http://mailchimp.com` and navigate to **Lists**. From here, select the **Signup forms** option from the dropdown next to your chosen client, as shown in the following screenshot:

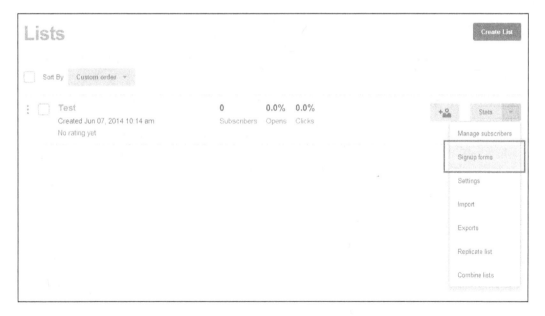

Next, click on the **Select** button beneath the **Embedded forms** option:

On the next screen, customize your form, and copy the content from the **Copy/paste onto your site** field. You'll need this for the next step.

Log in to your Magento site's administration panel, navigate to **CMS | Static Blocks**, and click on the **Add New Block** button at the top of the screen: enter a subtitle **Block Title** and enter `newsletter_mailchimp` in the **Identifier** field. Finally, ensure **Status** is set to **Enabled** and paste the subscription form code provided by MailChimp into the **Content** field, ensuring that you have used **Show / Hide Editor** button to disable the rich text editor before pasting the code in:

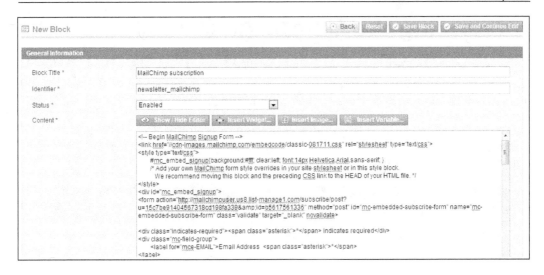

Click on the **Save Block** button to create this block. Next, you need to assign the new block to a region on your store; open your theme's `local.xml` file from `/app/design/frontend/default/m18/layout/`, and add the following highlighted code to the reference `name="right"` element within the `<default>` handle:

```
<default>
  <reference name="right">
    <block type="cms/block" name="cms_mailchimp">
      <action method="setBlockId">
        <block_id>newsletter_mailchimp</block_id>
      </action>
    </block>
  </reference>
</default>
```

Once you have saved this change, you will see the subscription box appear on the pages with the right-hand column layout assigned:

# Integrating the Campaign Monitor subscription form into your Magento store

Campaign Monitor is another popular e-mail newsletter system you may use to keep in touch with customers outside the realm of Magento's transactional e-mails.

Firstly, you will need the subscription form code from your Campaign Monitor list: log in to your Campaign Monitor account, and navigate to the **Lists & Subscribers** tab. Select a subscriber list from here:

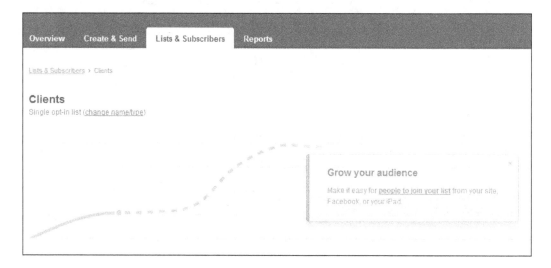

In the right-hand column of this screen, click on the **Grow your audience** option:

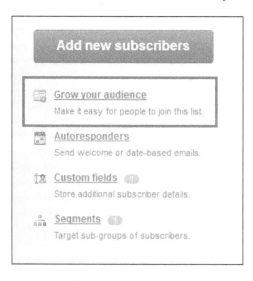

On the next screen, you will see an option for **Copy/paste a form to your site**:

Once you have customized the form to your liking, click on the **Get the code** button at the bottom of the screen:

Copy the code presented, and log in to your Magento store's administration panel. From here, navigate to **CMS | Static Blocks** and click on the **Add New Block** button at the top-right corner of your screen:

Click on the **Save Block** button and open your theme's `local.xml` file (present at `/app/design/frontend/default/m18/layout/`) to assign this block to the right-hand column using the following highlighted code:

```
<default>
  <reference name="right">
    <block type="cms/block" name="cms_campaignmonitor">
      <action method="setBlockId">
        <block_id>newsletter_campaignmonitor</block_id>
      </action>
    </block>
  </reference>
</default>
```

Refreshing your store once you have saved this change will display the subscription form for your Campaign Monitor account, allowing you to style it further should you wish to:

# Summary

This chapter introduced you to customizing Magento's many transactional e-mail templates, and helped give your store a personalized feel by e-mail as well as through your website. This chapter covered changing the e-mail template logo, altering colors and variables in Magento e-mail templates, adding static block content to your Magento e-mail templates, and creating a MailChimp or Campaign Monitor subscription block for use in your store.

Your Magento store should be well on its way to being customized now, though there is always work to be done!

# Index

## Symbols

**@font-face**
  using 115

## A

**AddThis**
  integrating 99-101
  URL 99
**advanced Magento theming**
  custom error page, creating 118
  custom print style sheet, adding 109, 110
  Google Web Fonts, using 115
  layered navigation, styling 116
  locales, using 112
  snippets, using 122
**Apple home icon, for mobile devices**
  adding, to Magento store 137, 138

## B

**base images 35**
**blank theme, Magento 14**
**blocks**
  content blocks 70
  deleting, from sidebar 83
  structural blocks 70
  types 70
**blocks, rearranging**
  block, reordering above all blocks 81
  block, reordering below all blocks 82
  block, repositioning below
    specific block 78-81
  in sidebar 77

## C

**Campaign Monitor**
  about 156
  URL for resources 141
  subscription form, integrating
    into Magento store 156-158
**Cap Store 23**
**cart page**
  styling 61-63
**checkout page**
  styling 64-68
**child theme 20**
**CMS tool**
  used, for changing page layout 72, 73
**color scheme, Magento e-mail templates**
  changing 145
**Comma Separate Values (CSV) file 113**
**content blocks 70**
**CSS media queries**
  adding, to style sheet 126-132
  used, for customizing Magento
    theme for devices 125
**custom 404 "not found" error page**
  content, altering 118-121
  creating 118
**custom print style sheet**
  adding, to Magento store 110

## D

**default Magento page template**
  changing, layout used 70

## Thank you for buying
# Learning Magento Theme Development

# About Packt Publishing

Packt, pronounced 'packed', published its first book "*Mastering phpMyAdmin for Effective MySQL Management*" in April 2004 and subsequently continued to specialize in publishing highly focused books on specific technologies and solutions.

Our books and publications share the experiences of your fellow IT professionals in adapting and customizing today's systems, applications, and frameworks. Our solution based books give you the knowledge and power to customize the software and technologies you're using to get the job done. Packt books are more specific and less general than the IT books you have seen in the past. Our unique business model allows us to bring you more focused information, giving you more of what you need to know, and less of what you don't.

Packt is a modern, yet unique publishing company, which focuses on producing quality, cutting-edge books for communities of developers, administrators, and newbies alike. For more information, please visit our website: www.packtpub.com.

# About Packt Open Source

In 2010, Packt launched two new brands, Packt Open Source and Packt Enterprise, in order to continue its focus on specialization. This book is part of the Packt Open Source brand, home to books published on software built around Open Source licenses, and offering information to anybody from advanced developers to budding web designers. The Open Source brand also runs Packt's Open Source Royalty Scheme, by which Packt gives a royalty to each Open Source project about whose software a book is sold.

# Writing for Packt

We welcome all inquiries from people who are interested in authoring. Book proposals should be sent to author@packtpub.com. If your book idea is still at an early stage and you would like to discuss it first before writing a formal book proposal, contact us; one of our commissioning editors will get in touch with you.

We're not just looking for published authors; if you have strong technical skills but no writing experience, our experienced editors can help you develop a writing career, or simply get some additional reward for your expertise.

## Magento Site Performance Optimization

ISBN: 978-1-78328-705-5          Paperback: 92 pages

Leverage the power of Magento to speed up your website

1.  Improve the performance of Magento by more than 70%.

2.  Master Magento caching techniques.

3.  Using a step-by-step approach, learn how to optimize Magento site performance.

## Magento Search Engine Optimization

ISBN: 978-1-78328-857-1          Paperback: 132 pages

Maximize sales by optimizing your Magento store and improving exposure in popular search engines like Google

1.  Optimize your store for search engines in other countries and languages.

2.  Enhance your product and category pages.

3.  Resolve common SEO issues within Magento.

Please check **www.PacktPub.com** for information on our titles

## [PACKT] open source
### PUBLISHING
community experience distilled

**Mastering Magento**
**Theme Design**

Create responsive themes using Bootstrap, the most widely used frontend framework

Andrea Saccà

PACKT open source

# Mastering Magento Theme Design

ISBN: 978-1-78328-823-6          Paperback: 310  pages

Create responsive themes using Bootstrap, the most widely used frontend framework

1.  Create an advanced responsive Magento theme based on the Bootstrap 3 framework.

2.  Configure your custom theme with the Magento Admin Panel.

3.  Create your theme from scratch using practical live coding examples.

**Magento Responsive**
**Theme Design**

Leverage the power of Magento to successfully develop and deploy a responsive Magento theme

Richard Carter

PACKT open source

# Magento Responsive Theme Design

ISBN: 978-1-78398-036-9          Paperback: 110 pages

Leverage the power of Magento to successfully develop and deploy a responsive Magento theme

1.  Build a mobile-, tablet-, and desktop-friendly e-commerce site.

2.  Refine your Magento store's product and category pages for mobile.

3.  Easy-to-follow, step-by-step guide on how to get up and running with Magento.

Please check **www.PacktPub.com** for information on our titles